GUITAR • VOCAL

STRUM & SING — CHRISTMAS SONGS

Lyrics, chord symbols and guitar chord diagrams for 40 songs

T0083307

ISBN 978-1-4950-6593-4

HAL•LEONARD®
CORPORATION

7777 W. BLUEMOUND RD. P.O. BOX 13819 MILWAUKEE, WI 53213

Visit Hal Leonard Online at
www.halleonard.com

CONTENTS

All I Want for Christmas Is My Two Front Teeth

Words and Music by
Don Gardner

D   E   A7   G   G#°7   F#7   Bm

Chorus 1

|D |E
All I want for Christmas is my two front teeth,
  |A7 |D |
My two front teeth, see my two front teeth.
| |E
Gee, if I could only have my two front teeth
    |A7 |D
Then I could wish you, "Merry Christmas."

Verse

‖G |G#°7 |
It seems so long since I could say,
|D   A7 |D   F#7 |
"Sister Susie sitting on a thistle."
|Bm | |E |A7   N.C.   ‖
  Ev'ry time I try to speak all I do is whistle. Sssss.

Chorus 2

|D |E

 All I want for Christmas is my two front teeth,

 |A7 |D |

My two front teeth, see my two front teeth.

| |G   G♯°7

Gee, if I could only have my two front teeth

 |D   A7 |D   ‖

Then I could wish you, "Merry Christmas."

Bridge

|G |G♯°7 |

 Good old Santa Claus and all his reindeer

|D   A7 |D

 They used to bring me lots of toys ___ and candy.

F♯7 |Bm |

 Gee but, but now when I go out and call,

| |

"Dancer, Prancer, Donner and Blitzen,"

| E |A7   N.C. ‖

None of them can understand ___ me. Ssssss.

Chorus 3

|D |E

 All I want for Christmas is my two front teeth,

 |A7 |D |

My two front teeth, see my two front teeth.

| |G   G♯°7

All I want for Christmas is my two front teeth

 |D A7 |D   N.C. | |

So I can wish you, "Merry Christmas." *Christ - mas. Christmas.*

| | |D   ‖

Oh, for goodness sakes. Happy New Year!

Baby, It's Cold Outside
from the Motion Picture NEPTUNE'S DAUGHTER

By Frank Loesser

D	Em	A7	Am7	D7	G	Gm	E7	B7
××○	○ ○○○	×○ ○	×○ ○	××○	○○○	×○ ×	○ ○○	× ○
1 3 2	2 3	2 3	2 1	2 1 3	2 1 3	2 3 4	2 1	2 1 3 4

Intro |D |Em   A7 |

Verse 1

‖D |
I really can't stay,

| | |
   (But baby it's cold outside!)

|Em   A7 |
I've got to go 'way.

| |Em   A7 |
   (But baby it's cold outside!)

|D |
This evening has been

| | |
   (Been hoping that you'd drop in.)

| | Am7 |
So ___ very nice.

| |D7 |
   (I'll hold your hands, ___ they're ___ just like ice.)

|G | |
My mother will start to worry

|
(Beautiful, what's your hurry?)

|Gm |
And father will be pacing the floor.

| | |
   (Listen to the fireplace roar!)

|**D** |
So really I'd better scurry,

| | | |
(Beautiful, please don't hurry.)

|**E7** |**A7**
Well, maybe just half a drink more.

| |
(Put some records on while I pour.)

|**D** |
The neighbors might think,

| |
(Baby, it's bad out there.)

|**Em** A7 |
Say, what's in this drink?

| |**Em** A7 |
(No cabs to be __ had out there.)

|**D** |
I wish I knew how

| | |
(Your eyes are like starlight now)

|**Am7** |
To __ break the spell.

| |**D7** |
(I'll take your hat, your hair looks swell.)

|**G** |
I ought to say "No, no, no, Sir!"

| | |
(Mind if I move in closer?)

|**E7** |
At least I'm gonna say that I tried.

|**A7** |
(What's the sense of hurting my pride.)

|**D** |
I really can't stay.

| |**B7**
(Oh, baby, don't hold __ out.)

|**E7** **A7** |**D** ||
Ah, but it's cold out - side.

Interlude |**D** |**Em** **A7** |
              |**D** |**Em** **A7**

Verse 2

```
 ‖D                   |
I simply must go.
 |           |              |
   (But baby it's cold outside!)
   |Em            A7   |
The answer is no!
 |              |E           A7   |
   (But baby it's cold outside!)
   |D              |
The welcome has been,
 |              |           |
   (How lucky that you dropped in.)
 |              |Am7       |
   So ___ nice and warm.
 |              |D7        |         |
   (Look out the win - dow __ at that storm.)
   |G            |
My sister will be sus - picious,
 |              |
(Gosh, your lips look deli - cious.)
   |Gm           |
My brother will be there at the door.
 |              |
(Waves upon a tropical shore!)
   |D            |
My maiden aunt's mind is  vicious.
 |              |       |
(Gosh, your lips are de   -    licious.)
   |E7              |A7   |
Well, maybe just a cigarette more.
 |              |
(Never such a blizzard before.)
```

```
 |D                        |
I've got to get home.

|              |              |
   (Baby, you'd freeze out there.)
   |Em                  A7   |
Say, can you lend me your comb?

|              |Em            A7   |
   (It's up to your __ knees out there.)
        |D                   |
You've really been grand,

|              |              |
   (I thrill when you touch my hand.)
     |              |Am7   |
But ___ don't you see,

|                    |D7              |
   (How can you do    this thing to me.)
        |G              |
There's bound to be talk to - morrow.

|              |              |
(Think of my life-long sorrow.)
 |E7                          |
At least there will be plenty implied.
|A7                          |
(If you caught pneu - monia and died.)
 |D              |
I really can't stay,

|                    |B7         |
   (Get over that old __ doubt.)
              |E7   |   |A7   |   |D   |        ‖
Ah, but it's cold    out   -    side.
```

Blue Christmas

Words and Music by
Billy Hayes and Jay Johnson

E   A   B7   E7   F#7   Bb°7

231   123   213 4   2 1   3 2 1   12 3

Intro

|E   A |E N.C. |

Verse 1

‖E | |B7 | |
I'll have a blue Christmas with - out you.

| | | |E | |
  I'll be so blue just thinking a - bout you.

| | |E7 |A | | |
  Decora - tions of red __ on a green Christmas tree

|F#7 | |B7 | N.C.
Won't be the same, dear, if you're not here with me.

Verse 2

‖E | |B7 | |
And when those blue snowflakes start fallin',

| | | |E | |
  That's when those blue mem - 'ries start callin'.

| | |E7 |A |Bb°7 |
  You'll be do - in' alright __ with your Christmas of white,

|B7 | |E | N.C.   ‖
But I'll have a blue, blue, blue, blue Christmas.

Interlude

|E | |B7 | | |
| | |E | |

Outro-Verse

‖E |E7 |A |Bb°7 |
You'll be doin' alright __ with your Christmas of white,

|B7 | | |E | ‖
But I'll have a blue, blue, blue, blue Christ - mas.

The Christmas Waltz

Words by Sammy Cahn
Music by Jule Styne

Intro | G | E7 | Am7 |

Verse | D7 || G | E7 | Am7 | D7

Frosted window panes,   candles gleaming in - side,

| G | E7 | Am7 |

Painted candy canes ___ on the tree.

| D7 | G | | Am7 | D7 | Gmaj7 | Em7

Santa's on his way, he's filled his sleigh with things,

| A7 | D7

Things for you and for me.

| G | E7 | Am7 | D7

It's that time of year   when the world falls in love.

| G | E7 | Am7 | D7

Ev'ry song you hear ___ seems to say:

| G | | Am7 | D7 | Dm6 | E7

"Merry Christmas, may your New Year dreams come true."

| A7 | D7 | G | E7

And this song of mine,   in three-quarter time,

| A7 | D7 | G | Am7 | D7 | G ||

Wishes you and yours   the same thing, too.

Caroling, Caroling

Words by Wihla Hutson
Music by Alfred Burt

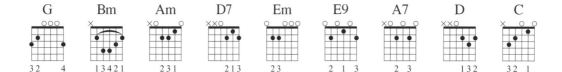

Verse 1

|G   Bm |G   Bm |
Caroling, caroling, now we go,

|Am   D7 |G   Em |
Christmas bells are ring - ing!

|Bm   E9 |Bm   E9 |
Caroling, caroling through the snow,

|Em   A7 |D |
Christmas bells are ringing!

|Am |D |
Joyous voices sweet and clear,

|G |Em |
Sing the sad of heart to cheer.

|C   G |D7   G |
Ding, dong, ding, dong,

|Am   D7 |G   ‖
Christmas bells are ringing!

Verse 2

```
|G      Bm  |G        Bm   |
```
Caroling, caroling through the town,
```
|Am      D7   |G    Em   |
```
Christmas bells are ring - ing!
```
|Bm      E9   |Bm    E9    |
```
Caroling, caroling up and down,
```
|Em      A7   |D        |
```
Christmas bells are ringing!
```
|Am              |D          |
```
Mark ye well the song we sing,
```
|G              |Em         |
```
Gladsome tidings now we bring.
```
|C    G   |D7  G      |
```
Ding, dong, ding, dong,
```
|Am      D7   |G          ||
```
Christmas bells are ringing!

Verse 3

```
|G      Bm  |G        Bm   |
```
Caroling, caroling, near and far,
```
|Am      D7   |G    Em   |
```
Christmas bells are ring - ing!
```
|Bm      E9   |Bm    E9    |
```
Following, following yonder star,
```
|Em      A7   |D        |
```
Christmas bells are ringing!
```
|Am              |D          |
```
Sing we all this happy morn,
```
|G              |Em         |
```
"Lo, the King of heav'n is born!"
```
|C    G   |D7  G      |
```
Ding, dong, ding, dong,
```
|Am      D7   |G          ‖
```
Christmas bells are ringing!

The Christmas Song
(Chestnuts Roasting on an Open Fire)

Music and Lyric by
Mel Tormé and Robert Wells

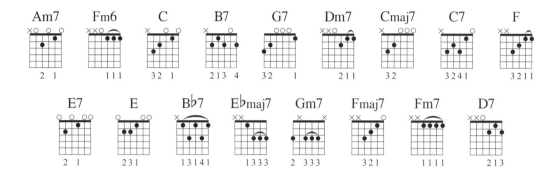

Intro

|Am7 Fm6 |C   B7 |

|C   G7 |C ||

Verse 1

|C   Dm7 |Cmaj7 G7 |
Chestnuts roasting on an open fire,

|C   C7 |F   E7 |
Jack Frost nipping at your nose,

|Am7 Fm6 |C   B7 |
Yuletide carols being sung by a choir,

|E   Bb7 |Ebmaj7 |
And folks dressed up like Eski - mos.

G7 |C   Dm7 |Cmaj7 G7 |
Ev'rybody knows a turkey and some mistletoe

|C   C7 |F   E7 |
Help to make the season bright.

|Am7 Fm6 |C   B7 |
Tiny   tots with their eyes all a - glow

|C   G7 |C |
Will find it hard to sleep to - night.

Bridge

‖ **Gm7 C7**   │ **Gm7   C7**
They know that San   -   ta's on his way;

│ **Gm7   C7**   │ **Fmaj7**
He's loaded lots of toys and goodies on his sleigh,

│ **Fm7   Fm6**   │ **E♭maj7**
And every mother's child ____ is gonna spy

│ **Am7   D7**   │ **Dm7   G7**
To see if reindeer really know how to fly.

Outro

‖ **C   Dm7**   │ **Cmaj7 G7**
And so I'm offering this simple phrase

│ **C   C7**   │ **F   E7**
To kids from one to ninety-two.

│ **Am7   Fm6**   │ **C   B7**
Al - though it's been said many times, many ways,

│ **C   G7** │ **C**   ‖
"Merry Christmas   to you."

Christmas Time Is Here

from A CHARLIE BROWN CHRISTMAS

Words by Lee Mendelson
Music by Vince Guaraldi

Gmaj7 D7♭9 F9#11 C#m7♭5 Bm7 Am7

D7sus4 Gmaj9 E♭maj7 A♭7♭5 E7 D13

Intro

| Gmaj7 | D7♭9 | Gmaj7 | D7♭9 ||

Verse 1

| Gmaj7 | F9#11 |
Christmas time is here,
| Gmaj7 | F9#11 |
Happiness and cheer.
| C#m7♭5 | Bm7 |
Fun for all that children call
| Am7 D7sus4 | Gmaj9 ||
Their fav'rite time of year.

Verse 2

| Gmaj7 | F9#11 |
Snowflakes in the air,
| Gmaj7 | F9#11 |
Carols ev'ry - where.
| C#m7♭5 | Bm7 |
Olden times and ancient rhymes
| Am7 D7sus4 | Gmaj9 ||
Of love and dreams to share.

Bridge

| E♭maj7 | A♭7♭5 |

Sleigh bells in the air,

| E♭maj7 | A♭7♭5 |

Beauty ev'ry - where.

| Bm7 | E7

Yuletide by the fireside

| Am7 | D13 ‖

And joyful mem'ries there.

Verse 3

| Gmaj7 | F9♯11 |

Christmas time is here,

| Gmaj7 | F9♯11 |

We'll be drawing near.

| C♯m7♭5 | Bm7

Oh, that we could always see

| Am7 | D7sus4 | Gmaj9 ‖

Such spirit through the year.

Bridge 2

Repeat Bridge 1

Verse 4

Repeat Verse 3

Do You Hear What I Hear

Words and Music by
Noel Regney and Gloria Shayne

C   Bb   Am   Em   F   G   E   G7

Intro

|C   Bb |C | Bb |C |

Verse 1

‖C   Bb |C |
Said the night wind to the little   lamb,

| | |
"Do you see what I see?

| Bb |C |
Way up in the sky, little   lamb,

| |
Do you see what I see?

|Am |Em
A star, a star, dancing in the night,

    |F   G |E   Am
With a tail as big as a kite,

    |F   G7 |C   Bb |C
With a tail as big as a kite."

Verse 2

|C   Bb |C |
Said the little lamb to the shepherd boy,

| | |
"Do you hear what I hear?

| Bb |C |
Ringing through the sky, shepherd boy,

| |
Do you hear what I hear?

|Am |Em
A song, a song, high above the tree,

    |F   G |E   Am
With a voice as big as the sea,

    |F   G7 |C |
With a voice as big as the sea."

Verse 3

```
        ‖C                   B♭  |C         |
```
Said the shepherd boy to the mighty king,
```
|                           |      |
```
"Do you know what I know?
```
|                    B♭  |C        |
```
In your palace warm, mighty king,
```
|                           |
```
Do you know what I know?
```
 |Am          |Em
```
A Child, a Child shivers in the cold;
```
      |F        G        |E    Am
```
Let us bring Him silver and gold,
```
      |F        G7        |C        |
```
Let us bring Him silver and gold."

Verse 4

```
         ‖C                   B♭  |C         |
```
Said the king to the people ev'ry - where,
```
|                      |      |
```
"Listen to what I say!
```
|                        B♭  |C        |
```
Pray for peace, people ev'ry - where,
```
|                 |
```
Listen to what I say!
```
 |Am               |Em
```
The Child, the Child, sleeping in the night,
```
      |F        G          |E    Am
```
He will bring us goodness and light,
```
      |F        G7          |C      B♭|C        |       B♭|C       ‖
```
He will bring us goodness and light."

Do You Want to Build a Snowman?

from FROZEN

Music and Lyrics by
Kristen Anderson-Lopez and Robert Lopez

(Capo 1st fret)

Asus4 D Dsus4 Gmaj7/A Dadd2 Aadd2/C♯ G/B Bm Am(add9) C/E

D/F♯ Gadd2 F♯m7 Dmaj7 C♯m7♭5 F♯7 E7 Em9 Gm6 Dsus2

B♭ D/A G5 G5/A A Am G E Dadd4 Gm7

Dm/F F Dm/A F♯m F♯sus²₄ A/C♯ C♯°7

Intro ‖: Asus4 D Dsus4 :‖ Asus4 D Dsus4 | Asus4 D Dsus4 |

(Little Anna:) *Elsa?*   *(Knocking)*

Verse 1

| Gmaj7/A   ‖ Dadd2 |
Do you want to build a snowman?

| | Aadd2/C♯ |
Come on, let's go and play!

| | G/B | Bm |
I never see you anymore. Come out the door!

| | Am(add9) C/E   D/F♯ |
It's like you've gone a - way.

| | Gadd2 |
We used to be best buddies,

| F♯m7   Dmaj7 |
And now we're not.

| C♯m7♭5   F♯7 | Bm |
I wish you would tell me why.

| E7   N.C. | Em9 |
Do you want to build a snowman?

| | Gm6 |
It doesn't have to be a snowman. (Little Elsa:) *Spoken: Go away, Anna.*

| ‖
(Little Anna:) *Sung:* Okay,

Interlude 1

|D Dsus4 Dsus2 |D Dsus4 Dsus2 |D Dsus4 Dsus2 |
Bye.

|D Dsus4 Dsus2 |B♭   D/A |B♭   D/A |

|D Dsus4 Dsus2 |D Dsus4 Dsus2 |G5 |

| G5/A |B♭ |

(Knocking)

Verse 2

|A   N.C.   ‖D |
  (**Young Anna:**) Do you want to build a snowman?

| |Aadd2/C♯ |
  Or ride our bikes around the halls?

| |G/B
  I think some company is overdue.

                |Bm |Am   N.C. |
I've started talking to the pictures on the walls. *Spoken: Hang in there, Joan!*

| |G |D/F♯
  Sung: It gets a little lonely, all these empty rooms,

  |F♯7 |Bm |E N.C. | ‖
Just watching the hours tick by.   *(Click tongue)*

Interlude 2

|B♭ | |Gm7 | | |

|B♭ | | | | |

|N.C. | | |

‖: D Dsus4 Dsus2 |D Dsus4 Dsus2 :‖Dadd4 |

| |Gm7 |Gm6 |Dm/F |

|A |Gm7 |Gm6 |Dm/F |

|F |Gm7 | |Dm/A |

| |B♭ | | | |

| |A | | | |

| |N.C. |

(Knocking) (**Anna:**) *Spoken:* Elsa?

Verse 3

                    | ‖**Dsus2** |
Sung: Please, I know you're in there.

         | |**Aadd2/C♯** |
People are asking where you've been.

         | |**G/B**
They say, "Have courage," and I'm trying to.

         |**Bm** |**F♯m** **F♯sus⅔** |
I'm right out here for you, just let me in.

|**F♯m** |**G** |**A/C♯** **D** |
  We only have each other, it's just you and me.

|**C♯m7♭5** **C♯°7**|**Bm** | |**E7** |
 What are we gonna do?

         | |**N.C.**   **D/F♯** |**G** |
  Do you want to build a snowman?

|**N.C.** **G** |**A** |**N.C.** | ‖

Outro

     |**N.C.** **Bm** |**G** |**N.C.** **Bm** |**G** |**N.C.(D)** ‖

Feliz Navidad

Music and Lyrics by
José Feliciano

Em7   A7   D   G

Intro | Em7 | A7 | D   G   ‖

                  | D N.C.   ‖ Em7 | A7
Chorus 1   Feliz Navi - dad.

                              | D |
                  Feliz Navi - dad.

                  | | Em7
                    Feliz Navi - dad.

                              | A7 | D |
                  Prospero año y felici - dad.

Chorus 2   *Repeat Chorus 1*

                  | ‖ G |
Verse   I want to wish you a Merry Christmas,

                  | A7 | D |
                    With lots of presents to make you happy.

                  | | G
                  I want to wish you a Merry Christmas

                              | A7 | D   G |
                  From the bottom of my heart.

                  | D | G |
                    I want to wish you a Merry Christmas,

                  | A7 | D |
                    With mistletoe and lots of cheer,

                  | | G
                  With lots of laughter through - out the years,

                              | A7 | D   G | D
                  From the bottom of my heart.

Chorus 3   *Repeat Chorus 1*

Chorus 4   *Repeat Chorus 1*

Frosty the Snow Man

Words and Music by
Steve Nelson and Jack Rollins

F	C	A7	Dm7	G7	C7
××	× ○	×○ ○ ○	××○	○○○	×
3 2 1 1	3 2 1	2 3	2 1 1	3 2 1	3 2 4 1

Cmaj7	Dm	G	Am	D
× ○○○	××○	○○○	×○ ○	××○
3 2	2 3 1	3 2 4	2 3 1	1 3 2

Intro |**F** |**C**   **A7** |**Dm7 G7** |**C**   **G7** ‖

Verse 1

|**C** |
 Frosty the snow man
    |**F** |**C**
Was a jolly, happy soul,
    |**F** |**C**   **A7**
With a corncob pipe and a button nose
     |**Dm7**   **G7** |**C**   **G7** |
And two eyes made out of coal.
|**C** |
 Frosty the snow man
   |**F** |**C**
Is a fairy tale they say.
     |**F** |**C**   **A7**
He was made of snow but the children know
    |**Dm7**   **G7** |**C**   **C7**
How he came to life one day.

Bridge 1

```
      ‖F                      |Cmaj7
There must have been some magic
      |Dm      G7      |C
In that old silk hat they found,
  |G                       |
For when they placed it on his head,
        |Am      D      |G
He be - gan to dance a - round.
```

Verse 2

```
G7 ‖C           |
Oh,   Frosty the snow man
      |F              |C
Was a - live as he could be,
      |F                    |C       A7
And the children say he could laugh and play
      |Dm7      G7      |C  G7   ‖
Just the same as you and me.
```

Verse 3

```
|C           |
 Frosty the snowman
        |F           |C
Knew the sun was hot that day,
      |F                    |C       A7
So he said, "Let's run and we'll have some fun
        |Dm7 G7      |C      G7   |
Now be - fore I melt a - way."
|C           |
 Down to the village
      |F           |C
With a broomstick in his hand,
        |F                    |C       A7
Running here and there all a - round the square,
        |Dm7      G7  |C   C7
Sayin', "Catch me if you can."
```

Bridge 2

‖**F** |**Cmaj7**
He led them down the streets of town
   |**Dm** **G7** |**C**
Right to the traffic cop.
     |**G**
And he only paused a moment when
  |**Am**   **D** |**G**
He heard him holler "Stop!"

Verse 4

G7 ‖**C** |
For   Frosty the snowman
      |**F** |**C**
Had to hurry on his way,
     |**F** |**C**   **A7**
But he waved goodbye, sayin', "Don't you cry,
   |**Dm7**   **G7** |**C** **G7** ‖
I'll be back a - gain some day."

Outro

|**C** |
 Thumpety thump thump,
| |
Thumpety thump thump,
| |**G7** |
Look at Frosty go.
| |
Thumpety thump thump,
| |
Thumpety thump thump,
| |**C**   ‖
Over the hills of snow.

Happy Holiday

from the Motion Picture Irving Berlin's HOLIDAY INN

Words and Music by
Irving Berlin

D6   Em7   A7   D   Bm7   E7   A   F#m7

Intro

|D6 | |Em7 |

Verse 1

|A7 ||D6 | |Em7 |A7
   Happy holiday,   happy holiday.
        | |D
While the merry bells keep ringing,
Bm7 |**Em7**   **A7** |**D**
May your ev'ry wish   come true.
    |D6 | |Em7 |A7
Happy holiday,   happy holiday.
     | |D
May the calendar keep bringing
Bm7 |**Em7**   **A7** |**D**   **E7**
Happy holidays   to you.

Verse 2

     ||A | |B7 |E7
Happy holiday,   happy holiday.
       | |A   F#m7
While the merry bells keep ringing,
     |Bm7   E7 |A
May your ev'ry wish   come true.
      | | |Bm7 |E7
Happy holiday,   happy holiday.
      | |A   F#m7
May the calendar keep bringing
     |Bm7   E7 |A ||
Happy holidays   to you.

Happy Xmas
(War Is Over)

Written by
John Lennon and Yoko Ono

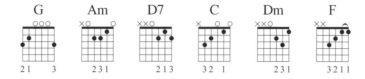

Verse 1

‖**G** |
So this is Christmas

| |**Am** |
And what have you done?

| | **D7** **Am** |
Another year over,

| **D7** |**G** |
And a new one just be - gun;

| |**C** |
And so this is Xmas,

| |**Dm** |
I hope you have fun,

| |**G** |
The near and the dear ones,

| |**C** |
The old and the young.

Chorus 1

| ‖**F** |
A merry, merry Christmas

| |**G** |
And a happy New Year.

| |**Dm** **F** |
Let's hope it's a good one

| **C** **D7** |
Without any fear.

Verse 2

```
|               ‖G        |
And so this is Christmas
|                    |Am      |
For weak and for strong,
|                    |D7        Am |
The rich and the poor ones,
|      D7      |G        |
The road is so long.
|                 |C          |
And so, happy Christmas
|                    |Dm      |
For black and for white,
|                    |G          |
For the yellow and red ones,
|              |C        |
Let's stop all the fights.
```

Chorus 2   *Repeat Chorus 1*

Verse 3

```
|              ‖G        |
And so this is Christmas
|                    |Am      |
And what have we done?
|              |    D7   Am |
Another year over,
|      D7          |G        |
And a new one just be - gun;
|              |C          |
And so this is Christmas,
|                    |Dm      |
We hope you have fun,
|                 |G          |
The near and the dear ones,
|              |C        |
The old and the young.
```

Chorus 3   *Repeat Chorus 1*

Outro

```
|G     |  |Am  |      |
War is over if you want it;
|D7  |Am  D7 |G    |      |D7  |Am  |G      ‖
War is o - ver   now.
```

Have Yourself a Merry Little Christmas

from MEET ME IN ST. LOUIS

Words and Music by
Hugh Martin and Ralph Blane

Intro

|C   **Am7** |**Dm7**   **G7** ||

Verse 1

|C   **Am7** |**Dm7**   **G7** |
Have your - self a merry little Christ - mas,

|C   **Am7** |**Gsus4**   **G** |
Let your heart be light.

|C   **Am7** |**Dm7** |
From now on our troubles will be

G7 |**E7**   **A7** |**D7**   **G7** ||
Out of sight.

Verse 2

|C   **Am7** |**Dm7**   **G7** |
Have your - self a merry little Christ - mas,

|C   **Am7** |**Gsus4**   **G** |
Make the Yuletide gay.

|C   **Am7** |
From now on

 |**Dm7**   **E7** |**Am** |**C7** ||
Our troubles will be miles a - way.

Bridge 1

|Fmaj7 Fm(maj7) |Em
Here we are as in olden days,

E♭°7 |Dm7   G7 |Cmaj7 |
   Happy golden days ____ of yore.

|F♯m7♭5 B7 |Em
Faithful   friends who are dear to us

A7 |G   D7 |Gsus4 G ‖
   Gather near to us ____ once more.

Verse 3

|C   Am7 |Dm7   G7 |
  Through the years we all will be togeth - er,

|C   Am7 |Gsus4 G |
  If the fates al - low.

|C   Am7 |Dm7
  Hang a shining star

        E7 |Am |
Upon the highest bough,

|C7 |Fmaj7   Am7
  And have your - self

|Dm7   G7 |C |C7   ‖
A merry little Christ - mas now.

Bridge 2

Repeat Bridge 1

Outro-Verse

|C   Am7 |Dm7   G7 |
  Through the years we all will be togeth - er,

|C   Am7 |Gsus4 G |
  If the fates al - low.

|C   Am7 |Dm7
  Hang a shining star

        E7 |Am |
Upon the highest bough,

|C7 |Fmaj7   Am7
  And have your - self

|Dm7   G7 |C | ‖
A merry little Christ - mas now.

Here Comes Santa Claus
(Right Down Santa Claus Lane)

Words and Music by
Gene Autry and Oakley Haldeman

G   G#°7   D   B7   Em   A7   D7

Intro |G   G#°7 |D B7 |Em A7 |D ||

Verse 1

|D | |
Here comes Santa Claus! Here comes Santa Claus!
|A7 | |
Right down Santa Claus Lane!
| |
Vixen and Blitzen and all his reindeer
   |D |D7 |
Are pulling on the rein.
|G   G#°7 |D   B7 |
Bells are ringing, children singing,
|Em A7 |D D7 |
All is merry and bright.
|G   G#°7 |D   B7 |
Hang your stockings and say your pray'rs,
    |Em   A7 |D ||
'Cause Santa Claus comes to - night.

Verse 2

|D | |
Here comes Santa Claus! Here comes Santa Claus!
|A7 | |
Right down Santa Claus Lane!
| |
He's got a bag that is filled with toys
   |D |D7 |
For the boys and girls a - gain.
|G   G#°7 |D B7 |
Hear those sleigh bells jingle, jangle,
|Em A7 |D D7 |
What a beautiful sight.
|G   G#°7 |D   B7 |
Jump in bed, cover up your head,
|Em A7 |D |
Santa Claus comes to - night.

Verse 3

|D | | |
 Here comes Santa Claus! Here comes Santa Claus!
|A7 | | |
 Right down Santa Claus Lane!
| | |
 He doesn't care if you're rich or poor,
      |D |D7 |
 For he loves you just the same.
|G G♯○7 |D B7 |
 Santa knows that we're God's children,
|Em A7 |D D7 |
 That makes ev'rything right.
|G G♯○7 |D B7 |
 Fill your hearts with a Christmas cheer,
      |Em A7 |D ‖
 'Cause Santa Claus comes to - night.

Verse 4

|D | | |
 Here comes Santa Claus! Here comes Santa Claus!
|A7 | | |
 Right down Santa Claus Lane!
| | |
 He'll come around when the chimes ring out,
      |D |D7 |
 Then it's Christmas morn a - gain.
|G G♯○7 |D B7 |
 Peace on earth will come to all
 |Em A7 |D D7 |
 If we just fol - low the light.
|G G♯○7 |D B7 |
 Let's give thanks to the Lord a - bove,
|Em A7 |D ‖
 Santa Claus comes to - night.

A Holly Jolly Christmas

Music and Lyrics by
Johnny Marks

Intro

|C |D7   G7 |C

Verse 1

‖C   Cmaj7 |C
Have a holly jolly   Christmas,
| C#°7 |G7 |
It's the best time of the year.
| |
I don't know if there'll be snow
| |C   G7
But have a cup of cheer.

Verse 2

‖C   Cmaj7 |C
Have a holly jolly   Christmas,
| C#°7 |G7 |
And when you walk down the street,
| |
Say hello to friends you know
| |C   C7 ‖
And ev'ryone you meet.

Bridge 1

|F |Em |
Oh, ho, the mistletoe

|F |C |
Hung where you can see,

|Dm |Am |
Somebody waits for you,

|D7 |G7
Kiss her once for me.

Verse 3

‖C   Cmaj7 |C
Have a holly jolly   Christmas,

| C♯°7 |G7 |
And in case you didn't hear,

| |C |
Oh, by golly, have a holly jolly

|D7   G7 |C   ‖
Christmas   this year.

Verse 4   *Repeat Verse 1*

Verse 5   *Repeat Verse 2*

Bridge 2   *Repeat Bridge 1*

Verse 6   *Repeat Verse 3*

(There's No Place Like)

Home For the Holidays

Words and Music by
Al Stillman and Robert Allen

Chord diagrams: C, F, A7, D7, G7, C7, G, Am7, C#°7, Dm7

Chorus 1

‖ **C** | **F** | **C** |
Oh, there's no place like home for the holidays,

| | | **A7** | **D7** | **G7**
'Cause no matter how far away you roam,

| **C** | **F** | **C** |
When you pine for the sunshine of a friendly gaze,

| **D7** | **G7** | | **C** | **C7**
For the holidays you can't beat home, sweet home.

Verse 1

‖ **F** | | | |
I met a man who lives in Tennessee, and he was headin'

| **C** | **G7** | | **C** |
For Pennsyl - vania and some homemade pumpkin pie.

| **C7** | **F** |
From Pennsyl - vania folks are trav'lin'

| | **C**
Down to Dixie's sunny shore;

| **G** | **Am7** **D7**
From At - lantic to Pa - ci - fic, gee,

| **G7** **C#°7** | **Dm7**
The traffic is ter - rific!

Chorus 2

G7　　　‖C　　　　　|F　　　　　|C　　　　　|
Oh, there's no place like home for the holidays,

|G7　　　　　|C　　　　|A7　　　　|D7　　|G7
　　'Cause no matter how far away you roam,

　　|C　　　|F　　　|C　　　　　|
If you want to be happy in a million ways,

|　　D7　　|G7　　　　|　　　　　　　|C　　　|
　　For the holidays you can't beat home, sweet home.

Chorus 3

Repeat Chorus 1

Verse 2

　　　　　　　‖F　　　　　　|
A home that knows your joy and laughter filled

　　|　　　　　　|C
With mem'ries by the score

　|G7　　　　　　|　　　　　　　|C　　　|
Is a home you're glad to welcome with your heart.

|C7　　　　|F　　　　|
　　From Cali - fornia to New England

　　　　|　　　　　　|C
Down to Dixie's sunny shore;

　　　　　|G　　　　　|Am7　D7
From At - lantic to Pa - cific,　gee,

　|G7　　C♯○7　|Dm7
The traffic is ter - rific!

Chorus 4

G7　　　‖C　　　　　|F　　　　　|C　　　　　|
Oh, there's no place like home for the holidays,

|G7　　　　|C　　　|A7　　　|D7　　|G7
　　'Cause no matter how far away you roam,

　　|C　　　|F　　　|C　　　|
If you want to be happy in a million ways,

D7　|G7　　　　|　　　　　|Dm7　|G7　|C　　|　　　‖
For the holidays you can't beat home,　sweet home.

37

I Saw Mommy Kissing Santa Claus

Words and Music by
Tommie Connor

Intro

|C |F   G7 |C |G7 ||

Verse 1

|C | |Em |Am |
I saw Mommy kissing Santa Claus
|C | |G7 |
Underneath the mistletoe last night.
| | | |
   She didn't see me creep
      |C |
Down the stairs to have a peep,
 |D7 | |G7 |
She thought that I was tucked up in my bedroom fast a - sleep.
  |C | |Em |Am |
Then I saw Mommy tickle Santa Claus,
|C | |F   A7 |Dm
 Underneath his beard so snowy white.
        |F |B7
Oh, what a laugh it would have been
 |C   A7 |Dm
If Daddy had only seen
G7 |C |F   G7 |C |G7 ||
Mommy kissing Santa Claus last night.

Verse 2

```
|C       |              |Em |Am    |
 I saw Mommy kissing Santa Claus
|C              |        |G7     |
 Underneath the mistletoe last night.
|       |        |        |
   She didn't see me creep
         |C            |
 Down the stairs to have a peep,
   |D7          |            |G7          |
 She thought that I was tucked up in my bedroom fast a - sleep.
     |C   |           |Em |Am     |
 Then I saw Mommy tickle Santa Claus,
|C            |              |F    A7    |Dm
 Underneath his beard so snowy white.
        |F              |B7
 Oh, what a laugh it would have been
 |C          A7 |Dm
 If Daddy had only seen
 G7      |C            |F    G7 |C    |      ‖
 Mommy kissing Santa Claus last  night.
```

I'll Be Home For Christmas

Words and Music by
Kim Gannon and Walter Kent

F6   Fm6   C   A7   Dm   Dm7   G7

Eb°7   Em7b5   A7b9   Am7   D7   A7

Intro

|F6 |Fm6 |C |A7 |
|Dm |Dm7 G7 |C |G7   ‖

Verse 1

|C |Eb°7 |Dm7 |G7 |
I'll be home for Christmas,

|Em7b5 A7b9 |Dm |G7 |
You can count on me.

|Fm6 |G7 |C |Am7 |
Please have snow and mistle - toe

   |D7 | |Dm7 |G7 |
And presents on the tree.

|C |Eb°7 |Dm7 |G7 |
Christmas Eve will find me

|Em7b5 |A7b9 |Dm | |
Where the lovelight gleams,

|F6 |Fm6 |C |A7 |
I'll be home for Christ - mas

   |Dm |Dm7 G7 |C |G7   ‖
If only   in   my   dreams.

Verse 2

|C |E♭°7 |Dm7 |G7 |
I'll be home for Christmas,

|Em7♭5 |A7♭9 |Dm |G7 |
You can   count on me.

|Fm6 |G7 |C |Am7
Please have snow and mistle - toe

  |D7 | |Dm7 |G7 |
And presents on the tree.

|C |E♭°7 |Dm7 |G7 |
Christmas Eve will find me

|Em7♭5 |A7♭9 |Dm | |
Where the lovelight gleams,

|F6 |Fm6 |C |A7 |
I'll be home for Christ - mas

 |Dm |Dm7 G7 |C | ‖
If only in   my   dreams.

It's Beginning to Look Like Christmas

By Meredith Willson

Am7   Bb°7   G   E7   D7   C   B7   D   A7   Em

Intro

|Am7 Bb°7 |G   E7 |Am7 D7 |

Verse 1

|G D7   ‖G   C |G |
     It's be - ginning to look a lot like Christmas,
| B7 |C   E7 |
Ev'ry - where you go.
    |Am7   D7 |
Take a look in the five and ten,
| G
Glistening once a - gain,
   |D   A7 |Am7 D7
With candy canes and silver lanes a - glow.
    |G   C |G |
It's be - ginning to look a lot like Christmas,
| B7 |C   E7
Toys in ev'ry store.
    |Am7   Bb°7
But the prettiest sight to see
   |G   E7
Is the holly that will be
   |Am7 D7 |G
On your own   front door.

Bridge

```
        ‖ B7
A pair of hopalong boots

And a pistol that shoots
      | Em                        |
Is the wish of Barney and Ben.
| A7
 Dolls that will talk

And will go for a walk
      | D
Is the hope of Janice and Jen.
       | D7
And Mom and Dad can hardly wait
      |
For school to start again.
```

Verse 2

```
        ‖ G             C    | G           |
It's be - ginning to look a lot like Christmas,
|         B7          | C    E7
Ev'ry - where you go.
            | Am7              D7   |
There's a tree in the grand ho - tel,
|                        G
One in the park as well,
      | D              A7            | Am7    D7
The sturdy kind that doesn't mind the snow.
          | G             C    | G           |
It's be - ginning to look a lot like Christmas,
|         B7          | C    E7
Soon the bells will start.
          | Am7                    B♭°7
And the thing that will make them ring
      | G              E7
Is the carol that you sing
            | Am7  D7  | G           ‖
Right with - in      your heart.
```

Jingle Bell Rock

Words and Music by
Joe Beal and Jim Boothe

(Capo 3rd fret)

C   Cmaj7   G7   C#°7   Dm   G7#5

C7   F   F#°7   D7   A7   Fm

Intro
|C   Cmaj7 |C | |G7 ||

Verse 1
|C   Cmaj7 |C |
Jingle-bell, jingle-bell, jingle-bell rock,
| C#°7 |Dm   G7 |
Jingle-bell swing and jingle-bells ring.
|Dm   G7 |Dm   G7 |
Snowin' and blowin' up bushels of fun,
|Dm |G7#5 ||
Now the jingle hop has begun.

Verse 2
|C   Cmaj7 |C |
Jingle-bell, jingle-bell, jingle-bell rock,
| C#°7 |Dm   G7 |
Jingle bells chime in jingle-bell time.
|Dm   G7 |Dm   G7 |
Dancin' and prancin' in Jingle Bell Square
|Dm   G7 |C   C7 |
In the frosty air.

|| **F** | **F#°7**

Bridge 1   What a bright time, it's the right time,

|**C** |

To rock the night a - way.

|**D7** | |

Jingle-bell time is a swell time

|**G7 N.C.** | ||

To go glidin' in a one-horse sleigh.

|**C**   **Cmaj7** |**C** |

Verse 3   Giddy-ap, jingle horse pick up your feet,

| |**A7** |

Jingle around the clock.

|**F** |**Fm** |

Mix and mingle in a jinglin' beat,

|**D7**   **G7** |**C** ||

That's the jingle-bell rock.

Verse 4   *Repeat Verse 2*

Bridge 2   *Repeat Bridge 1*

|**C**   **Cmaj7** |**C** |

Verse 5   Giddy-ap, jingle horse pick up your feet,

| |**A7** |

Jingle around the clock.

|**F** |**Fm** |

Mix and mingle in a jinglin' beat,

|**D7**   **G7** |

That's the jingle-bell,

|**D7**   **G7** |

That's the jingle-bell,

|**D7**   **G7** |**C** | ||

That's the jingle-bell rock.

Let It Snow! Let It Snow! Let It Snow!

Words by Sammy Cahn
Music by Jule Styne

G   D7   Bm7   A7   Am   E7   D   D#°7   Em   B7

Verse 1

|G   D7 |G
Oh, the weather out - side is frightful,

|Bm7 A7 |D7
But the fire is so de - lightful,

|Am   E7 |Am
And since we've no place to go,

|D7 |G
Let it snow! Let it snow! Let it snow!

Verse 2

‖G   D7 |G
It doesn't show signs of stopping,

|Bm7   A7 |D7
And I brought some corn for popping,

|Am   E7 |Am
The lights are turned way down low,

|D7 |G
Let it snow! Let it snow! Let it snow!

Bridge

‖D | D#°7
When we finally kiss good - night,

|Em   A7 |D
How I'll hate going out in the storm.

| |B7 |
But if you'll really hold me tight,

|E7   A7 |D   D7
All the way home I'll be warm.

Verse 3

‖G D7 |G
The fire is slowly dying

|Bm7   A7 |D7
And, my dear, we're still good-bye-ing,

|Am   E7 |Am
But as long as you love me so,

|D7 |G   ‖
Let it snow! Let it snow! Let it snow!

Mary, Did You Know?

Words and Music by
Mark Lowry and Buddy Greene

(Capo 1st fret)

Dm   C   Gm7   A7sus4   A   Gm   Asus4

Gm11   F   C/E   C6   A7   Bb/D   C/D

Intro

|Dm |C |Gm7 |A7sus4   A |

|Dm |C |Gm7 |

Verse 1

|A7sus4   ‖Dm |C

     Mary, did you know that your ba - by boy

|Gm |Asus4

Would one day walk on wa - ter?

A |Dm |C

Mary did you know that your ba - by boy

|Gm |Asus4   A

Would save our sons and daugh - ters?

|Gm11 |C

Did you know ____ that your ba - by boy

|F   C/E |Dm   C6

Has come to make ____ you new?

|Gm7 |

This child ____ that you deliv - ered

|A7sus4 |A7

Will soon deliver you.

Verse 2

```
        ‖Dm                |C
Mary, did you know that your ba - by boy
   |Gm               |Asus4
Will give sight to a blind ___ man?
A         |Dm               |C
Mary, did you know that your ba - by boy
     |Gm              |Asus4        A
Would calm a storm with His ___ hand?
           |Gm11            |C
Did you know ___ that your ba - by boy
    |F              C/E    |Dm    C6
Has walked where an - gels trod,
          |Gm7                    |
And when you kissed your little ba - by,
      |A7sus4              |A7
You've kissed the face of God?
                  |Dm      |C       |Gm7    |
Oh, Mary, did you know?
|A7sus4   A         |Dm      |C      |Gm7       |
      Mary, do you know?
```

Bridge

```
|A7sus4   A   ‖B♭/D           |C/D
      The       blind will see, the deaf will hear,
   |Dm         C/D     |B♭/D
The dead will live ___ again,
   |                |C/D
The lame will leap, the dumb will speak
   |Dm            |Asus4       |
The praises of the Lamb.
```

Verse 3

|A   ‖Dm |C
   Oh, Mary, did you know that your ba - by boy

 |Gm |Asus4
Is Lord of all crea - tion?

A |Dm |C
Mary, did you know that your ba - by boy

 |Gm |Asus4   A
Will one day rule the na - tions?

         |Gm11 |C
Did you know ____ that your ba - by boy

 |F   C/E |Dm   C6
Was heaven's per - fect Lamb,

         |Gm7 |
And the sleep - ing child you're hold - ing

     |Asus4 |A |Dm |C |Gm7 |Asus4   A   ‖
Is the great   I   Am?

Outro |Dm |C |Gm7 |A7sus4 |

                    |A |Dm | | ‖

The Little Drummer Boy

Words and Music by Harry Simeone,
Henry Onorati and Katherine Davis

A   E   D

chord diagrams

Intro

|A | ||

Rum pum, rum pum.

Verse 1

|A | | | |

Come, they told me, pa rum pum pum pum,

| | | | |

Our newborn King to see, pa rum pum pum pum.

|E | | | |

Our finest gifts we bring, pa rum pum pum pum,

| |A |D |

To lay be - fore the King, pa rum pum pum pum,

|A |E | |

Rum pum pum pum, rum pum pum pum.

|A | | |

So, to honor Him, pa rum pum pum pum,

| | | | ||

When we come.

Verse 2

|A | | | | |
Baby Jesu, pa rum pum pum pum,

| | | | | |
  I am a poor boy, too, pa rum pum pum pum.

|E | | | | |
  I have no gift to bring, pa rum pum pum pum,

| |A |D |
  That's fit to give our King, pa rum pum pum pum,

|A |E | |
 Rum pum pum pum, rum pum pum pum.

|A | | | |
 Shall I play for You, pa rum pum pum pum,

| | | | ||
On my drum?

Verse 3

|A | | | |
 Mary nodded, pa rum pum pum pum.

| | | | |
  The ox and lamb kept time, pa rum pum pum pum.

|E | | | |
  I played my drum for Him, pa rum pum pum pum.

| |A |D |
  I played my best for Him, pa rum pum pum pum,

|A |E |A |E |
 Rum pum pum pum, rum pum pum pum.

|A | | | |
 Then He smiled at me, pa rum pum pum pum,

| | | | ||
Me and my drum.

Little Saint Nick

Words and Music by
Brian Wilson and Mike Love

G C/E G/D Am7 D7 Gmaj7 G6 G#°7

G7 C Dsus4 D F A E7

Intro

| G   C/E G/D C/E | G   C/E G/D C/E |

| Am7 |
Ooh.

| D7 | G | |
Merry Christmas, Saint Nick.
               (Christmas comes this time each year.)

| Am7 | D7
Ooh.

Verse 1

‖ Am7   D7 | Am7   D7
Well, way up north where the air gets cold,

| G   Gmaj7 | G6   G#°7
There's a tale about Christmas that you've all been told.

| Am7   D7 | Am7   D7
And a real famous cat all dressed up in red,

| G   Gmaj7 | G6   G7
And he spends his whole year workin' out on his sled.

Chorus 1

‖ C |
It's the little Saint Nick. (Little Saint Nick.)

| Am7 | Dsus4 D
It's the little Saint Nick. (Little Saint   Nick.)

Verse 2

   ‖Am7   D7 |Am7   D7
Just a little bob - sled, we call it Old Saint Nick,

      |G   Gmaj7 |G6   G♯°7
But she'll walk a to - boggan with a four-speed stick.

      |Am7   D7 |Am7   D7
She's a candy-apple red with a ski for a wheel,

      |G   Gmaj7 |G6   G7
And when Santa hits the gas, man, just watch her peel.

Chorus 2   *Repeat Chorus 1*

Bridge

|C | |
 Run, run, reindeer.

|F |
 Run, run, reindeer.

| |C | |
Oh, run, run, reindeer.

|A
 Run, run, reindeer.

     | N.C.
He don't miss no one.

Verse 3

     ‖Am7   D7 |Am7   D7
And haulin' through the snow at a fright'nin' speed

      |G   Gmaj7 |G6   G♯°7
With a half a dozen deer with Rudy to lead.

      |Am7   D7 |Am7   D7
He's gotta wear his goggles 'cause the snow really flies,

      |G   Gmaj7 |G6   G7
And he's cruisin' ev'ry pad with a little surprise.

Chorus 3

      ‖C |
It's the little Saint Nick. (Little Saint Nick.)

     |G |G♯°7   ‖
It's the little Saint Nick. (Little Saint Nick.) Ah.

‖:Am7   D7 |Am7   D7 |
                Merry   Christmas,

|G   Gmaj7 |G♯°7   :‖ *Repeat to fade*
 Saint Nick.   Ah.
(Christmas comes this time each year.)

Merry Christmas, Darling

Words and Music by
Richard Carpenter and Frank Pooler

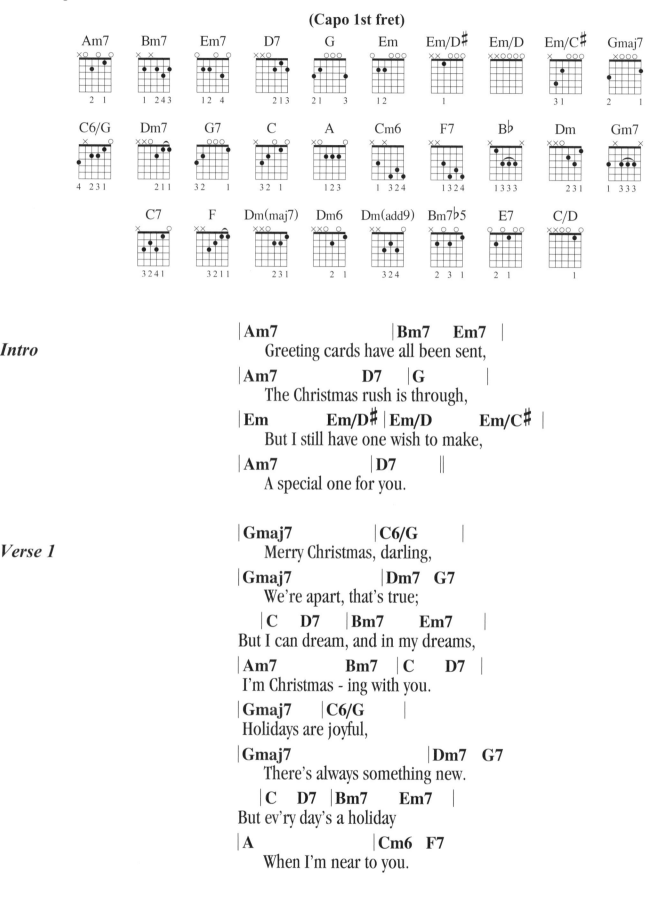

(Capo 1st fret)

Intro

|**Am7** |**Bm7**   **Em7** |
Greeting cards have all been sent,

|**Am7**   **D7** |**G** |
The Christmas rush is through,

|**Em**   **Em/D♯** |**Em/D**   **Em/C♯** |
But I still have one wish to make,

|**Am7** |**D7**   ‖
A special one for you.

Verse 1

|**Gmaj7** |**C6/G** |
Merry Christmas, darling,

|**Gmaj7** |**Dm7** **G7** |
We're apart, that's true;

|**C** **D7** |**Bm7**   **Em7** |
But I can dream, and in my dreams,

|**Am7**   **Bm7** |**C**   **D7** |
I'm Christmas - ing with you.

|**Gmaj7** |**C6/G** |
Holidays are joyful,

|**Gmaj7** |**Dm7** **G7** |
There's always something new.

|**C** **D7** |**Bm7**   **Em7** |
But ev'ry day's a holiday

|**A** |**Cm6** **F7** |
When I'm near to you.

Bridge 1

‖**B♭**   **C**
The lights on my tree
|**Am7**   **Dm** |
I wish you could see,
|**Gm7**   **C7** |**F**
  I wish it ev'ry day.
  |**Dm**   **Dm(maj7)** |
The logs on the fire
|**Dm7**   **Dm6** |
 Fill me with de - sire
|**G**   **Am7**|**Bm7** **Am7**
   To see you and to say…

Verse 2

D7 ‖**Gmaj7** |**C6/G** |
That I wish you a merry Christmas,
|**Gmaj7** |**Dm(add9)** **G7**
  Happy New Year, too.
  |**C**   **D7** |**Bm7**   **Em7** |
I've just one wish on this Christmas Eve;
|**Am7**   **D7** |**G** **F7** ‖
  I wish I were with you.

Bridge 2   *Repeat Bridge 1*

Verse 3

D7 ‖**Gmaj7** |**C6/G** |
That I wish you a merry Christmas,
|**Gmaj7** |**Dm(add9)** **G7**
  Happy New Year, too.
  |**C**   **D7** |**Bm7**   **Em7** |
I've just one wish on this Christmas Eve;
|**Am7**   **D7** |**Bm7♭5** **E7**|
  I wish I were with you.
|**Am7**   **D7** |**G** |**Am7** |**C/D** |**Gmaj7**‖
  I wish I were with you.

Mistletoe and Holly

Words and Music by Frank Sinatra,
Dok Stanford and Henry W. Sanicola

A   E7   C°7   Bm7   Dm7   G7   Cmaj7

G#m7   C#7   F#maj7   F#m7   B7   C#+   F#7

Intro

|: A | E7   :|

Verse 1

| A   E7 | A
Oh, by gosh, by golly,
             | C°7 | Bm7   E7 |
It's time for mistle - toe and holly,
| A   C°7 | E7 |
Tasty pheasants, Christmas presents,
| Bm7   E7 | A ||
Countrysides covered with snow.

Verse 2

| A   E7 | A
Oh, by gosh, by jingle,
             | C°7 | Bm7   E7 |
It's time for carols and Kris Kringle,
| A   C°7 | E7 |
Over - eating, merry greetings
| Bm7   E7 | A ||
From rela - tives you don't know.

Bridge

```
|Dm7 G7          |Cmaj7        |
 Then  comes that big night,
|Dm7      G7     |Cmaj7        |
 Giving the tree the trim,
|G♯m7     C♯7    |F♯maj7       |
 You'll hear voices by starlight
|B7              |E7        ||
 Singing a yuletide hymn.
```

Verse 3

```
|A       E7      |A
 Oh, by gosh, by golly,
                 |        C°7  |Bm7     E7  |
 It's time for mistle - toe  and holly,
|A     C°7  |E7                |
 Fancy ties   an' granny's pies an'
|Bm7            E7  |C+    F♯7
 Folks stealin' a kiss or two
         |B7              |E7        |A       |        ||
 As they whisper, "Merry Christmas to you."
```

The Most Wonderful Time of the Year

Words and Music by
Eddie Pola and George Wyle

(Capo 3rd fret)

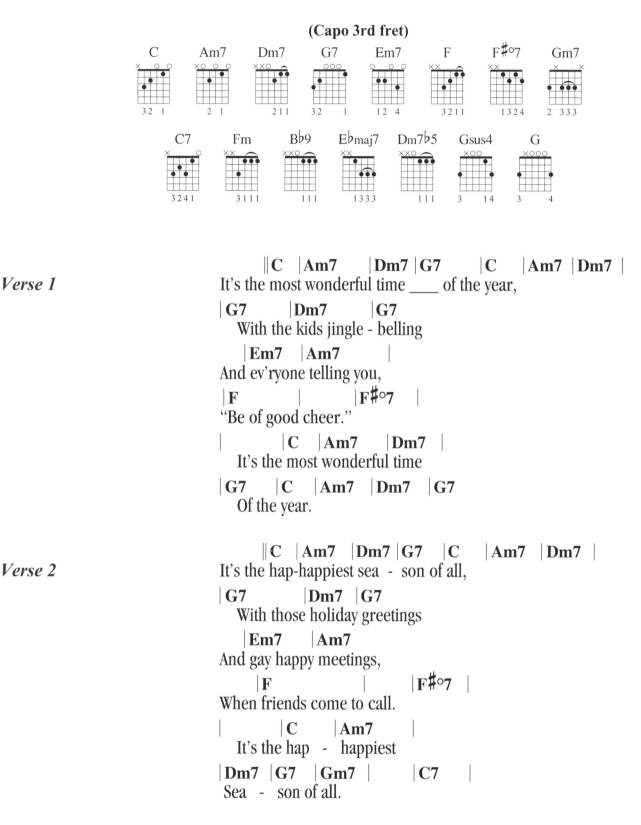

Verse 1

```
          ‖C  |Am7    |Dm7 |G7       |C    |Am7  |Dm7  |
```
It's the most wonderful time ___ of the year,
```
|G7      |Dm7      |G7    |
```
With the kids jingle - belling
```
  |Em7    |Am7       |
```
And ev'ryone telling you,
```
|F       |        |F#°7   |
```
"Be of good cheer."
```
|        |C  |Am7    |Dm7    |
```
It's the most wonderful time
```
|G7    |C   |Am7  |Dm7  |G7   |
```
Of the year.

Verse 2

```
          ‖C  |Am7   |Dm7 |G7   |C    |Am7    |Dm7  |
```
It's the hap-happiest sea - son of all,
```
|G7      |Dm7  |G7    |
```
With those holiday greetings
```
  |Em7    |Am7     |
```
And gay happy meetings,
```
      |F        |        |F#°7   |
```
When friends come to call.
```
|        |C  |Am7    |
```
It's the hap - happiest
```
|Dm7  |G7  |Gm7  |    |C7   |
```
Sea - son of all.

Bridge

```
|              ‖F          |F#°7
```
There'll be parties for hosting,
```
      |C          |Am7
```
Marsh - mallows for toasting
```
  |Dm7   |G7        |C          |
```
And caroling out in the snow.
```
|              |Fm          |B♭9
```
There'll be scary ghost stories
```
    |E♭maj7    |
```
And tales of the glories
```
  |Dm7♭5    |              |Gsus4   |      |      |
```
Of Christmases long, long a - go.

Verse 3

```
|G  N.C. ‖C   |Am7      |Dm7 |G7        |C       |Am7   |Dm7  |
```
It's the most wonderful time ___ of the year.
```
|G7         |Dm7         |G7
```
There'll be much mistle - toeing
```
    |Em7         |Am7
```
And hearts will be glowing
```
    |F              |      |F#°7   |
```
When loved ones are near.
```
|         |C   |Am7      |Dm7      |
```
It's the most wonderful time,
```
|G7         |C   |Am7      |Dm7      |
```
Yes, the most wonderful time,
```
|G7         |C   |Am7      |Dm7      |
```
Oh, the most wonderful time
```
|         |G7   |        |C       |
```
Of   the year.
```
|         |      |      ‖
```

My Favorite Things
from THE SOUND OF MUSIC

Lyrics by Oscar Hammerstein II
Music by Richard Rodgers

Verse 1

|**Em** | | | |
Raindrops on roses and whiskers on kittens,
|**Cmaj7** | | | |
Bright copper kettles and warm woolen mittens,
|**Am7** |**D7** |**G** |**C** |
Brown paper packages tied up with strings,
|**G** |**C** |**F♯m7♭5**|**B7** |**Em** |
These are a few of my favorite things.
| | | | |
Cream-colored ponies and crisp apple strudels,
|**Cmaj7** | | | |
Doorbells and sleighbells and schnitzel with noodles,
|**Am7** |**D7** |**G** |**C** |
Wild geese that fly with the moon on their wings,
|**G** |**C** |**F♯m7♭5**|**B7** |**E** ||
These are a few of my favorite things

Verse 2

|E | | | |
Girls in white dresses with blue satin sashes,

|A | | | |
Snowflakes that stay on my nose and eye - lashes,

|Am7 |D7 |G |C |
Silver white winters that melt into springs,

|G |C |F♯m7♭5 |B7 |
These are a few of my favorite   things.

|Em | |F♯m7♭5 | B7 |
  When the dog bites,   when the bee stings,

|Em | |C |
  When I'm feeling sad,

| |C | |A7 |
  I simply re - member my favorite things

  |G |C/D | |D7 |G | |C | |G |D7 |G   ‖
And then I don't feel   so bad.

Nuttin' for Christmas

Words and Music by
Sid Tepper and Roy C. Bennett

G   D7   C   A7   Em   Am   E7

Intro

| G | D7 | G | |

Verse 1

| D7 ‖ G | C   G |
    I broke my bat on Johnny's head;

| A7   D7 | G |
 Somebody snitched on me.

| | C   G |
 I hid a frog in sister's bed;

| A7   D7 | G |
 Somebody snitched on me.

| | C | |
 I spilled some ink on Mommy's rug,

| D7 | G | |
 I made Tommy eat a bug,

| Em | A7 | |
 Bought some gum with a penny slug;

| D7 | G |
 Somebody snitched on me.

Chorus 1

‖ G | | | | |
Oh, I'm gettin' nuttin' for Christmas.

| D7 | | | | |
Mommy and Daddy are mad.

| G | | | |
I'm gettin' nuttin' for Christmas,

| D7 | | G | |
'Cause I ain't been nuttin' but bad.

Verse 2

```
 ‖G           |C      G      |
I put a tack on teacher's chair;
|A7        D7          |G
 Somebody snitched on me.
 |              |C      G      |
I tied a knot in Susie's hair;
|A7        D7          |G
 Somebody snitched on me.
 |              |C              |
I did a dance on Mommy's plants,
|D7              |G              |
 Climbed a tree and tore my pants,
|Em          |A7              |
 Filled the sugar bowl with ants;
|D7              |G
 Somebody snitched on me.
```

Chorus 2   *Repeat Chorus 1*

Verse 3

```
 ‖G           |C      G      |
I won't be seeing Santa Claus;
|A7        D7          |G
 Somebody snitched on me.
  |              |C      G      |
He won't come visit me be - cause
|A7        D7          |G              |
 Somebody snitched on me.
 |              |C              |
 Next year I'll be  going straight,
|D7              |G              |
 Next year I'll be good, just wait,
|Em          |A7              |
 I'd start now, but it's too late;
|D7              |G
 Somebody snitched on me.
```

Chorus 3   *Repeat Chorus 1*

Outro

```
    ‖Am                  |E7
So you better be good, what - ever you do,
    |Am              |E7              |
'Cause if you're bad I'm warning you,
|Am      |D7      |G      |        ‖
 You'll get nuttin' for Christmas.
```

Rockin' Around the Christmas Tree

Music and Lyrics by
Johnny Marks

C	Am	F	G7	Em	D7	Dm
x ○ ○	x○ ○	x x	○○○	○ ○○○	x x○	x x○
3 2 1	2 3 1	3 2 1 1	3 2 1	1 2	2 1 3	2 3 1

Intro |C |Am |F |G7   ‖

Verse 1

|C |
 Rockin' around the Christmas tree
      |G7 | |
At the Christmas party hop.
| |
Mistletoe hung where you can see,
      | |C |
Ev'ry couple tries to stop.
| |
Rockin' around the Christmas tree,
      |G7 | |
Let the Christmas spirit ring.
| |
Later we'll have some pumpkin pie
        | |C   ‖
And we'll do some carol - ing.

Bridge 1

   |**F** | |**Em** | |
You will get a sentimental feeling when you hear
|**Am** | |
Voices singing "Let's be jolly,
|**D7** **N.C.** |**G7** ||
Deck the halls with boughs of holly!"

Verse 2

|**C** |
Rockin' around the Christmas tree,
     |**G7** | |
Have a happy holiday.
| |
Ev'ryone dancing merrily
    | |**C** ||
In the new old-fashioned way.

Verse 3   *Repeat Verse 1*

Bridge 2   *Repeat Bridge 1*

Verse 4

|**C** |
Rockin' around the Christmas tree,
     |**G7** | |
Have a happy holiday.
| |
Ev'ryone dancing merrily
   | | **Dm**   **G7**|**C** |**Am** |**F** **Dm** |**C** ||
In the new old-fash - ioned   way.

Rudolph the Red-Nosed Reindeer

Music and Lyrics by
Johnny Marks

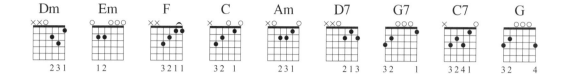

Intro

|Dm   Em |F   C |
You know Dasher and Dancer and Prancer and Vixen,
|Dm   Em |F   C |
Comet and Cupid and Donner and Blitzen,
|Am |
But do you re - call
              |D7 |G7   ‖
The most famous reindeer of all?

Verse 1

|C | |
Rudolph, the red-nosed reindeer
| |G7 |
Had a very shiny nose,
| | |
And, if you ever saw it,
| |C |
You would even say it glows.

| | |
All of the other reindeer
| |G7 |
Used to laugh and call him names,
| | |
They never let poor Rudolph
| |C   C7   ‖
Join in any reindeer games.

Bridge 1

|F |C |
Then one foggy Christmas Eve
|G7 |C |
Santa came to say,
|G | |
"Rudolph, with your nose so bright,
|Am   D7 |G7   ‖
Won't you guide my sleigh tonight?"

Verse 2

|C | |
Then how the reindeer loved him
| |G |
As they shouted out with glee:
| | |
"Rudolph, the red-nosed reindeer,
| |C |
You'll go down in histo - ry!"

Verse 3   *Repeat Verse 1*

Bridge 2   *Repeat Bridge 1*

Verse 4

|C | |
Then how the reindeer loved him
| |G |
As they shouted out with glee:
| | |
"Rudolph, the red-nosed reindeer,
| | |C | ‖
You'll go down in histo - ry!"

Santa Baby

By Joan Javits,
Phil Springer and Tony Springer

(Capo 1st fret)

C	Am7	D7	G7	Dm7	C6	E7	A7	Db9b5

Intro

|C   Am7 |D7 G7 |C   Am7 |D7 G7 ||

Verse 1

|C   Am7 |D7   G7 |C   Am7 |
Santa Baby, just ____ slip a sable under the tree ____ for me.
|D7   G7 |C   Am7
Been an awful good girl, ____ Santa Baby,
|Dm7   G7 |C   Am7 |D7 G7 ||
So, hurry down the chimney tonight.

Verse 2

|C   Am7 |D7   G7 |C   Am7 |
Santa Baby, a fifty-four con - vertible too, ____ light blue.
|D7   G7 |C   Am7
I'll wait up for you dear, ____ Santa Baby,
|Dm7   G7 |C   Am7 |D7 G7 C6 ||
So hurry down the chimney tonight.

Bridge 1

|E7 | |
Think of all the fun I've missed.
|A7 | |
Think of all the fellas that I ____ haven't kissed.
|D7 |
Next year I could be   just as good
|G7 N.C. | ||
If you   check off my Christmas list.

Verse 3

|C   Am7 |D7   G7 |C   Am7 |
Santa Baby, I want a yacht and really that's not ___ a lot.

|D7   G7 |C   Am7
Been an angel all year, ___ Santa Baby.

  |Dm7   G7 |C |Dm7   D♭9♭5 ‖
So, hurry down the chimney tonight.

Verse 4

|C   Am7 |D7   G7 |C   Am7 |
Santa Honey,   one little thing ___ I really need; ___ the deed

|D7   G7 |C   Am7
To a platinum mine, ___ Santa Baby.

  |Dm7   G7 |C |Dm7   D♭9♭5 ‖
So, hurry down the chimney tonight.

Verse 5

|C   Am7 |D7   G7 |C   Am7 |
Santa Cutie, and fill my stocking with a duplex ___ and checks.

|D7   G7 |C   Am7
Sign your "X" on the line, ___ Santa Cutie,

  |Dm7   G7 |C   Am7 |D7 G7 C6   ‖
And hurry down the chimney tonight.

Bridge 2

|E7 | |
      Come and trim my Christmas tree

|A7 | |
 With some decorations bought at   Tiffany.

|D7 | |
 I really do be - lieve in you.

|G7 N.C. | ‖
 Let's see if you be - lieve in me.

Verse 6

|C   Am7 |D7   G7 |C   Am7 |
Santa Baby, for - got to mention one little thing: ___ a ring.

|D7   G7 |C   Am7 |
I don't mean on the phone, ___ Santa Baby.

 |Dm7   G7 |C Am7 |
So, hurry down the chimney tonight.

|Dm7   G7 |C Am7 |
Hurry down the chimney tonight.

|Dm7 G7 |D♭9♭5 C6   ‖
Hurry   tonight.

Santa Claus Is Comin' to Town

Words by Haven Gillespie
Music by J. Fred Coots

C   Am   Dm   G7   F   Fm6   C7   D7   G

Intro

| C Am | Dm G7 | C Am | Dm G7

Verse 1

‖ C | F |
You better watch out, you better not cry,

| C | F   Fm6 |
Better not pout, I'm telling you why.

| C Am | Dm   G7 | C Am | Dm G7
Santa Claus is comin' ___ to town.

Verse 2

‖ C | F |
He's making a list and checking it twice,

| C | F   Fm6 |
Gonna find out who's naughty and nice.

| C Am | Dm   G7 | C | F C
Santa Claus is comin' ___ to town.

Bridge 1

‖ C7 | F
He sees you when you're sleeping.

| C7 | F
He knows when you're a - wake.

| D7 | G
He knows if you've been bad or good,

| D7 | G
So be good for goodness sake.

Verse 3

```
G7    ‖C                    |F                   |
Oh, you better watch out, you better not cry,
|C                |F        Fm6  |
 Better not pout, I'm telling you why.
|C   Am  |Dm    G7  |C  Am |Dm  G7
 Santa Claus is comin' ___ to town.
```

Verse 4

```
       ‖C                |F              |
With little tin horns and little toy drums,
|C                |F        Fm6  |
 Rooty toot toots and rummy tum tums.
|C   Am  |Dm    G7  |C  Am |Dm  G7  ‖
 Santa Claus is comin' ___ to town.
```

Verse 5

```
|C                |F              |
 Curly head dolls that cuddle and coo,
|C                |F        Fm6  |
 Elephants, boats and kiddie cars, too.
|C   Am  |Dm    G7  |C  |F   C
 Santa Claus is comin' ___ to town.
```

Bridge 2

```
     ‖C7          |F
The kids in Girl-and-Boyland
    |C7        |F       |
Will have a jubi - lee.
|D7                |G
   They're gonna build a Toyland town
       |D7                |G
All a - round the Christmas tree.
```

Outro-Verse

```
G7    ‖C                    |F                   |
Oh, you better watch out, you better not cry,
|C                |F        Fm6  |
 Better not pout, I'm telling you why.
|C   Am  |Dm  G7  |
 Santa Claus is comin',
|C   Am  |Dm  G7  |
 Santa Claus is comin',
|C   Am  |Dm    G7  |C  F   |
 Santa Claus is comin' ___ to town.
|C  N.C.              C   ‖
   He's comin' to town.
```

Silver Bells

from the Paramount Picture THE LEMON DROP KID

Words and Music by
Jay Livingston and Ray Evans

C C7 F Fm G7 Dm D7

Intro

| C | C7 | F | Fm |

| C | G7 | C | |

Verse 1

| G7 ‖ C | C7

City sidewalks, busy sidewalks,

| F | Dm

Dressed in holiday style;

| G7 | | C | G7

In the air there's a feeling of Christmas.

| C | C7

Children laughing, people passing,

| F | D7

Meeting smile after smile,

| G7 | | C | ‖

And on ev'ry street corner you hear:

Chorus 1

```
|C              |              |
 Silver bells. (Silver bells.)
|F              |              |
 Silver bells. (Silver bells.)
|G7            |          |C          |G7      |
 It's Christmas time in the city.
|C              |              |
 Ring-a-ling. (Ring-a-ling.)
|F              |              |
 Hear them ring. (Hear them ring.)
|G7          |          |C      |      |G7
 Soon it will be Christmas day.
```

Verse 2

```
              ‖C                |C7
Strings of street lights, even stoplights
       |F           |Dm
Blink a bright red and green
       |G7          |          |C          |G7
As the shoppers rush home with their treasures.
         |C                |C7
Hear the snow crunch, see the kids bunch,
       |F           |Dm
This is Santa's big scene,
       |G7                |C      |      ‖
And a - bove all this bustle you hear:
```

Chorus 2

Repeat Chorus 1

Sleigh Ride

Music by Leroy Anderson
Words by Mitchell Parish

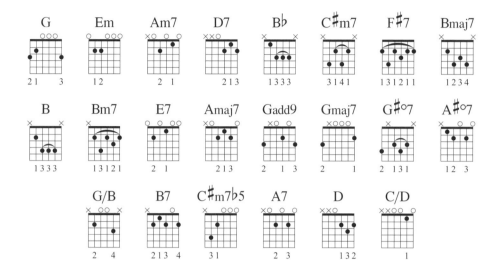

Intro

|G Em |Am7 D7 |G |

Verse 1

| N.C. ||G   Em |
Just hear those sleigh bells jingling,

|Am7   D7 |G   Em |
Ring-ting-tingling, too.

|Am7   D7 |G   Em |
Come on, it's lovely weather

    |Am7   D7 |G |
For a sleigh ride to - gether with you.

|B♭   D7 |G   Em |
Out - side the snow is falling

    |Am7   D7 |G   Em |
And friends are calling "Yoo hoo."

|Am7   D7 |G   Em |
Come on, it's lovely weather

    |Am7   D7 |G |
For a sleigh ride to - gether with you.

Bridge

| ‖C#m7 | F#7 |
Giddy yap, giddy yap, giddy yap, let's go.

|Bmaj7 | |
Let's look at the show.

|C#m7 | F#7 |B |
We're riding in a wonder - land of snow.

| |Bm7 | E7 |
Giddy yap, giddy yap, giddy yap, it's grand,

|Amaj7 | |
Just holding your hand.

|Am7 | |D7   Am7 |D7 |
We're gliding a - long with a song of a wintery fairy - land.

Verse 2

            ‖G   Em |Am7 D7 |G   Em |
Our cheeks are nice and rosy, and comfy cozy are we.

|Am7   D7 |G   Em |Am7   D7 |G |
We're snuggled up to - gether like two birds of a feather would be.

|B♭   D7 |G   Em |Am7 D7 |G   Em |
Let's take that road be - fore us and sing a chorus or two.

|Am7   D7 |G   Em
Come on, it's lovely weather

   |Am7   D7 |G |
For a sleigh ride to - gether with you.

Verse 3

| ‖Gadd9 | |Gmaj7
There's a birthday party at the home of Farmer Gray.

  | | | |
It'll be the perfect ending of a perfect day.

  |G#°7 |Am7   A#°7 |G/B   B7 |Em   C#m7♭5
We'll be singing the songs we love to sing with - out a single stop,

  |B |C#m7   F#7 |B |
At the fireplace while we watch the chestnuts pop.

|D7
Pop! Pop! Pop!

Verse 4

‖**Gadd9** | | |**Gmaj7**
There's a happy feeling nothing in the world can buy,

          | | | |
When they pass around the coffee and the pumpkin pie.

     |**G♯°7** |**Am7** **A♯°7** |**G/B** **B7** |**Em** **A7** |
It'll nearly be like a picture print by Curri - er and Ives.

|**D**   **C/D** |**D**   **C/D** |**D**
     These wonder - ful   things are the things we re - member

     C/D |**D7**
All thru our lives!

Verse 5

               ‖**G**   **Em** |
Just hear those sleigh bells jingling,

|**Am7**   **D7** |**G** **Em** |
 Ring-ting-tingling, too.

|**Am7**   **D7** |**G**   **Em**
     Come on, it's lovely weather

     |**Am7**   **D7** |**G** |
For a sleigh ride to - gether with you.

|**B♭**   **D7** |**G**   **Em**
     Out - side the snow is falling

     |**Am7**   **D7** |**G** **Em** |
And friends are calling "Yoo hoo."

|**Am7**   **D7** |**G**   **Em**
     Come on, it's lovely weather

     |**Am7**   **D7** |**G** | ‖
For a sleigh ride to - gether with you.

Snowfall

Lyrics by Ruth Thornhill
Music by Claude Thornhill

$$D6 \quad Dmaj7 \quad D_9^6 \quad Dm_9^6 \quad D \quad D7 \quad A9 \quad D_9^{6*} \quad Bm9/E$$

$$E7 \quad A6 \quad E\flat7sus4 \quad A\flat13 \quad D\flat6 \quad A7 \quad A7/D \quad A7\sharp5/D$$

Intro

‖: D6 | :‖

Verse

| Dmaj7 D§ | | Dmaj7 Dm§ | |
Snowfall, ___   softly,

| D   Dmaj7 | D7 A9 | Dmaj7 D§* | |
Gently ___   drift down.

| Dmaj7 D§ | | Dmaj7 Dm§ | |
Snowflakes ___   whisper

| D   Dmaj7 | D7 A9 | Dmaj7 D§* | ‖
'Neath my ___   window.

Bridge

| Bm9/E E7 | A6 |
Cov - 'ring trees

| E♭m7sus4 A♭13 | D♭6 |
Mist - y white,

| Bm9/E E7 | A6 |
Vel - vet breeze

| E♭m7sus4 A♭13 | D♭6 A7 ‖
'Round   my door - step.

Outro

| Dmaj7 D§ | | Dmaj7 Dm§ | |
Gently, ___   softly,

| D   Dmaj7 | D7 A9 | Dmaj7 D§* | |
Silent ___   snowfall!

| A7/D | A7♯5 | D§*   ‖

This Christmas

Words and Music by
Donny Hathaway and Nadine McKinnor

Bbmaj7   Am   Abmaj7   Ebmaj7   F   Fmaj7   Dm9   Dm7

C13sus4   Am7   D9   Gm7   C7sus4   B7#11   Eb9   Bm7b5

Intro

‖: **Bbmaj7 Am   Abmaj7 Bbmaj7 Ebmaj7 F** | :‖
| **Bbmaj7 Am   Abmaj7 Bbmaj7 Ebmaj7 F** | ‖

Verse 1

| **Fmaj7** |
Hang all the mistletoe.
| **Dm9** | **Ebmaj7** |
I'm gonna get to know you better
| **Dm7   C13sus4** |
This Christ - mas.
| **Fmaj7** |
And as we trim the tree,
| **Dm9** | **Ebmaj7** |
How much fun it's gonna to - gether
| **Dm7   C13sus4**
This Christ - mas.

Chorus 1

‖ **Am7** | **D9**
The fireside is blazing bright.
| **Gm7** | **C7sus4**
We're carolin' through the night
| **F   B7#11** | **Bbmaj7   Eb9** |
And this Christmas   will   be a   very special
| **Am7   Dm7** | **Bm7b5   B7#11** ‖
Christmas   for me.

Interlude 1 | B♭maj7 Am   A♭maj7 B♭maj7 E♭maj7 F | |
| B♭maj7 Am   A♭maj7 B♭maj7 E♭maj7 F | ||

Verse 2

| Fmaj7 |
Presents and cards are here.

| Dm9 |E♭maj7 |
   My world is filled with cheer and you,

| Dm7   C13sus4 ||
   This Christ - mas.

| Fmaj7 |
 And as I look around

| Dm9 |E♭maj7 |
 Your eyes outshine the town, they do,

| Dm7   C13sus4 ||
   This Christ - mas.

Chorus 2

| Am7 |D9
 Fireside is blazing bright.

  | Gm7 |C7sus4
We're carolin' through the night

    |F   B7♯11 |B♭maj7 E♭9 |
And this Christmas   will   be a   very special

| Am7   Dm7 |Bm7♭5 B7♯11 ||
 Christmas   for   me.

Interlude 2   *Repeat Interlude 1*

Piano Solo   *Repeat Verse 1 (Instrumental)*

Chorus 3

```
 ‖Am7                    |D9
The fireside is blazing bright.
        |Gm7                      |C7sus4
We're carolin' through the night
         |F       B7♯11 |B♭maj7  E♭9          |
And this Christmas    will   be a      very special
|Am7      Dm7   |Bm7♭5  B7♯11     |
 Christmas      for   me.
|B♭maj7  Am   A♭maj7  B♭maj7  E♭maj7  F   |
|                     |B♭maj7  Am   A♭maj7  B♭maj7  E♭maj7  F   |
     Merry Christmas.
|
     Shake your hand,
                 |B♭maj7  Am   A♭maj7  B♭maj7  E♭maj7  F   |
Shake your hand now.
|
     Wish your brother
             |B♭maj7  Am   A♭maj7  B♭maj7  E♭maj7  F   |
Merry Christmas
|             |B♭maj7  Am   A♭maj7  B♭maj7  E♭maj7  F   |            ‖
     All over the land ___ now.
```

Outro

```
‖:B♭maj7  Am   A♭maj7  B♭maj7  E♭maj7  F   |            :‖  Repeat and fade
```

White Christmas

from the Motion Picture Irving Berlin's HOLIDAY INN

Words and Music by
Irving Berlin

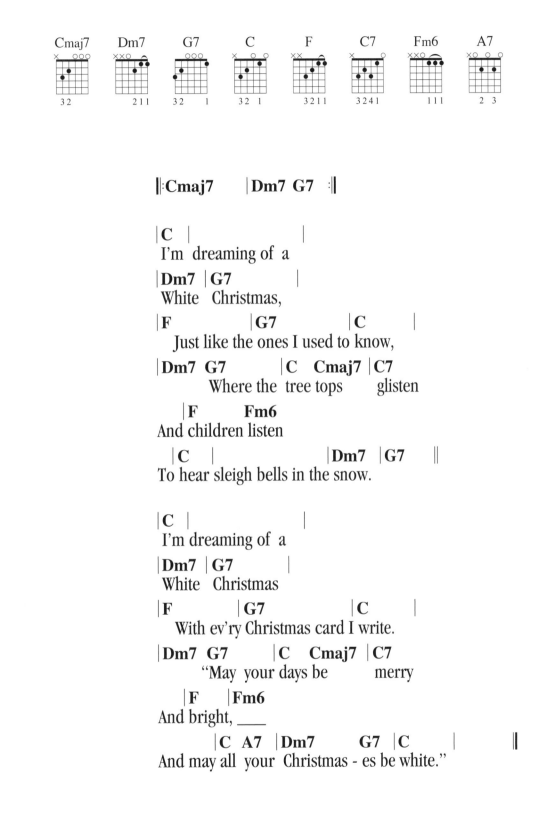

Intro ‖: **Cmaj7** |**Dm7 G7** :‖

Verse 1

|**C** | |
I'm dreaming of a
|**Dm7** |**G7** |
White   Christmas,
|**F** |**G7** |**C** |
    Just like the ones I used to know,
|**Dm7 G7** |**C Cmaj7** |**C7**
    Where the tree tops   glisten
      |**F**   **Fm6**
And children listen
      |**C** | |**Dm7** |**G7**   ‖
To hear sleigh bells in the snow.

Verse 2

|**C** | |
 I'm dreaming of a
|**Dm7** |**G7** |
White   Christmas
|**F** |**G7** |**C** |
    With ev'ry Christmas card I write.
|**Dm7 G7** |**C Cmaj7** |**C7**
    "May your days be   merry
    |**F** |**Fm6**
And bright, ___
      |**C A7** |**Dm7**   **G7** |**C** | ‖
And may all your Christmas - es be white."

Winter Wonderland

Words by Dick Smith
Music by Felix Bernard

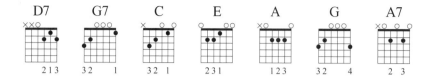

Intro

| D7   G7 | C

Verse 1

|| C |
Sleigh bells ring, are you list'nin'?
| G7 |
In the lane snow is glist'nin'.
| | | |
A beautiful sight, we're happy tonight,
| D7   G7 | C
Walkin' in a winter wonder - land.

Verse 2

|| C |
Gone a - way is the bluebird,
| G7 |
Here to stay is a new bird.
| | |
He sings a love song as we go along
| D7   G7 | C ||
Walkin' in a win - ter wonder - land.

Bridge 1

| E   A | E |
In the meadow we can build a snowman
| A | E |
And pretend that he is Parson Brown.
| G   C | G
He'll say, "Are you married?" We'll say, "No man!
| A7   D7 | G7
But you can do the job when you're in town!"

Verse 3

    ‖ **C** |
Later on __ we'll con - spire,

| |**G7** |
  As we dream by the fire,

 | | | |
To face unafraid __ the plans that we've made

|**D7**   **G7** |**C** |
 Walkin' in a winter wonder - land.

Verse 4   *Repeat Verse 1*

Verse 5   *Repeat Verse 2*

Bridge 2

|**E**   **A** |**E** |
 In the meadow we can build a snowman

| **A** |**E** |
 And pretend that he's a circus clown.

|**G**   **C** |**G**
 We'll have lots of fun with mister snowman

 |**A7**   **D7** |**G7**
Un - til the other kiddies knock him down.

Outro-Verse

    ‖ **C** |
Later on we'll con - spire,

| |**G7** |
  As we dream by the fire,

 | | | |
To face unafraid the plans that we've made

|**D7**   **G7** |**C** **A7** |
 Walkin' in a win - ter wonder - land.

|**D7**   **G7** |**C**   ‖
 Walkin' in a winter wonder - land.

STRUM & SING

Lyrics, chord symbols, and guitar chord diagrams for your favorite songs.

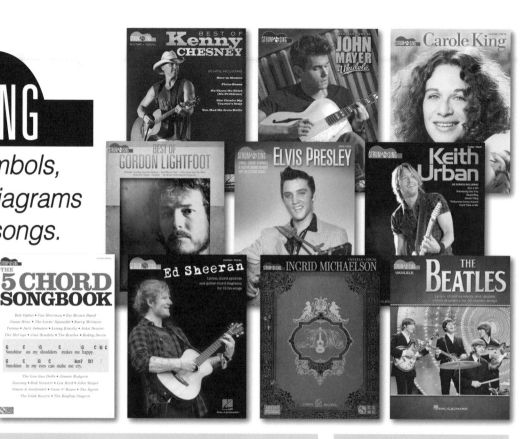

GUITAR

ACOUSTIC CLASSICS
00191891 .... $14.99

ADELE
00159855 .... $12.99

SARA BAREILLES
00102354 .... $12.99

THE BEATLES
00172234 .... $16.99

BLUES
00159335 .... $12.99

ZAC BROWN BAND
02501620 .... $14.99

COLBIE CAILLAT
02501725 .... $14.99

CAMPFIRE FOLK SONGS
02500686 .... $14.99

CHART HITS OF 2014-2015
00142554 .... $12.99

CHART HITS OF 2015-2016
00156248 .... $12.99

BEST OF KENNY CHESNEY
00142457 .... $14.99

CHRISTMAS SONGS
00171332 .... $14.99

KELLY CLARKSON
00146384 .... $14.99

COFFEEHOUSE SONGS FOR GUITAR
00285991 .... $14.99

LEONARD COHEN
00265489 .... $14.99

JOHN DENVER COLLECTION
02500632 .... $12.99

DISNEY
00233900 .... $16.99

EAGLES
00157994 .... $12.99

EASY ACOUSTIC SONGS
00125478 .... $14.99

THE 5 CHORD SONGBOOK
02501718 .... $12.99

FOLK SONGS
02501482 .... $10.99

FOLK/ROCK FAVORITES
02501669 .... $12.99

FOUR CHORD SONGS
00249581 .... $14.99

THE 4 CHORD SONGBOOK
02501533 .... $12.99

THE 4-CHORD COUNTRY SONGBOOK
00114936 .... $15.99

THE GREATEST SHOWMAN
00278383 .... $14.99

HAMILTON
00217116 .... $14.99

JACK JOHNSON
02500858 .... $17.99

ROBERT JOHNSON
00191890 .... $12.99

CAROLE KING
00115243 .... $10.99

BEST OF GORDON LIGHTFOOT
00139393 .... $14.99

DAVE MATTHEWS BAND
02501078 .... $10.95

JOHN MAYER
02501636 .... $10.99

INGRID MICHAELSON
02501634 .... $10.99

THE MOST REQUESTED SONGS
02501748 .... $12.99

JASON MRAZ
02501452 .... $14.99

PRAISE & WORSHIP
00152381 .... $12.99

ELVIS PRESLEY
00198890 .... $12.99

QUEEN
00218578 .... $12.99

ROCK AROUND THE CLOCK
00103625 .... $12.99

ROCK BALLADS
02500872 .... $9.95

ROCKETMAN
00300469 .... $17.99

ED SHEERAN
00152016 .... $14.99

THE 6 CHORD SONGBOOK
02502277 .... $12.99

CAT STEVENS
00116827 .... $14.99

TAYLOR SWIFT
00159856 .... $12.99

THE 3 CHORD SONGBOOK
00211634 .... $10.99

TODAY'S HITS
00119301 .... $12.99

TOP CHRISTIAN HITS
00156331 .... $12.99

TOP HITS OF 2016
00194288 .... $12.99

KEITH URBAN
00118558 .... $14.99

THE WHO
00103667 .... $12.99

YESTERDAY
00301629 .... $14.99

NEIL YOUNG – GREATEST HITS
00138270 .... $14.99

UKULELE

THE BEATLES
00233899 .... $16.99

COLBIE CAILLAT
02501731 .... $10.99

COFFEEHOUSE SONGS FOR UKULELE
00138238 .... $14.99

JOHN DENVER
02501694 .... $10.99

FOLK ROCK FAVORITES FOR UKULELE
00114600 .... $12.99

THE 4-CHORD UKULELE SONGBOOK
00114331 .... $14.99

JACK JOHNSON
02501702 .... $19.99

JOHN MAYER
02501706 .... $10.99

INGRID MICHAELSON
02501741 .... $12.99

THE MOST REQUESTED SONGS
02501453 .... $14.99

JASON MRAZ
02501753 .... $14.99

SING-ALONG SONGS
02501710 .... $15.99

HAL•LEONARD®

www.halleonard.com
Visit our website to see full song lists.

Prices, content, and availability subject to change without notice.

Guitar Chord Songbooks

Each 6" x 9" book includes complete lyrics, chord symbols, and guitar chord diagrams.

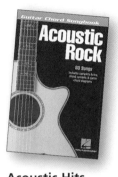
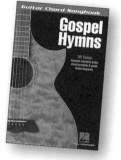
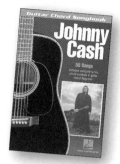
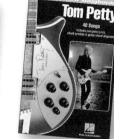

Acoustic Hits
00701787 . . . . $14.99

Acoustic Rock
00699540 . . . . $19.99

Alabama
00699914 . . . . $14.95

The Beach Boys
00699566 . . . . $17.99

The Beatles (A-I)
00699558 . . . . $17.99

The Beatles (J-Y)
00699562 . . . . $17.99

Bluegrass
00702585 . . . . $14.99

Johnny Cash
00699648 . . . . $17.99

Children's Songs
00699539 . . . . $16.99

Christmas Carols
00699536 . . . . $12.99

Christmas Songs – 2nd Edition
00119911 . . . . $14.99

Eric Clapton
00699567 . . . . $16.99

Classic Rock
00699598 . . . . $16.99

Coffeehouse Hits
00703318 . . . . $14.99

Country
00699534 . . . . $14.99

Country Favorites
00700609 . . . . $14.99

Country Hits
00140859 . . . . $14.99

Country Standards
00700608 . . . . $12.95

Cowboy Songs
00699636 . . . . $15.99

Creedence Clearwater Revival
00701786 . . . . $15.99

Jim Croce
00148087 . . . . $14.99

Crosby, Stills & Nash
00701609 . . . . $12.99

John Denver
02501697 . . . . $16.99

Neil Diamond
00700606 . . . . $17.99

Disney – 2nd Edition
00295786 . . . . $17.99

The Best of Bob Dylan
14037617 . . . . $17.99

Eagles
00122917 . . . . $16.99

Early Rock
00699916 . . . . $14.99

Folksongs
00699541 . . . . $14.99

Folk Pop Rock
00699651 . . . . $15.99

40 Easy Strumming Songs
00115972 . . . . $15.99

Four Chord Songs
00701611 . . . . $14.99

Glee
00702501 . . . . $14.99

Gospel Hymns
00700463 . . . . $14.99

Grand Ole Opry®
00699885 . . . . $16.95

Grateful Dead
00139461 . . . . $14.99

Green Day
00103074 . . . . $14.99

Guitar Chord Songbook White Pages
00702609 . . . . $29.99

Irish Songs
00701044 . . . . $14.99

Michael Jackson
00137847 . . . . $14.99

Billy Joel
00699632 . . . . $16.99

Elton John
00699732 . . . . $15.99

Ray LaMontagne
00130337 . . . . $12.99

Latin Songs
00700973 . . . . $14.99

Love Songs
00701043 . . . . $14.99

Bob Marley
00701704 . . . . $14.99

Bruno Mars
00125332 . . . . $12.99

Paul McCartney
00385035 . . . . $16.95

Steve Miller
00701146 . . . . $12.99

Modern Worship
00701801 . . . . $16.99

Motown
00699734 . . . . $17.99

Willie Nelson
00148273 . . . . $15.99

Nirvana
00699762 . . . . $16.99

Roy Orbison
00699752 . . . . $16.99

Peter, Paul & Mary
00103013 . . . . $14.99

Tom Petty
00699883 . . . . $15.99

Pink Floyd
00139116 . . . . $14.99

Pop/Rock
00699538 . . . . $16.99

Praise & Worship
00699634 . . . . $14.99

Elvis Presley
00699633 . . . . $15.99

Queen
00702395 . . . . $14.99

Red Hot Chili Peppers
00699710 . . . . $17.99

The Rolling Stones
00137716 . . . . $17.99

Bob Seger
00701147 . . . . $12.99

Carly Simon
00121011 . . . . $14.99

Sting
00699921 . . . . $14.99

Taylor Swift
00263755 . . . . $16.99

Three Chord Acoustic Songs
00123860 . . . . $14.99

Three Chord Songs
00699720 . . . . $14.99

Two-Chord Songs
00119236 . . . . $14.99

U2
00137744 . . . . $14.99

Hank Williams
00700607 . . . . $16.99

Stevie Wonder
00120862 . . . . $14.99

Neil Young–Decade
00700464 . . . . $15.99

Prices, contents, and availability subject to change without notice.

Visit Hal Leonard online at **www.halleonard.com**

Celebrate Christmas
WITH YOUR GUITAR AND HAL LEONARD

THE BEST CHRISTMAS GUITAR FAKE BOOK EVER – 2ND EDITION
INCLUDES TAB

Over 150 Christmas classics for guitar. Songs include: Blue Christmas • The Chipmunk Song • Frosty the Snow Man • Happy Holiday • A Holly Jolly Christmas • I Saw Mommy Kissing Santa Claus • I Wonder As I Wander • Jingle-Bell Rock • Rudolph, the Red-Nosed Reindeer • Santa Bring My Baby Back (To Me) • Suzy Snowflake • Tennessee Christmas • and more.
00240053 Melody/Lyrics/Chords $25.00

THE BIG CHRISTMAS COLLECTION FOR EASY GUITAR

Includes over 70 Christmas favorites, such as: Ave Maria • Blue Christmas • Deck the Hall • Feliz Navidad • Frosty the Snow Man • Happy Holiday • A Holly Jolly Christmas • Joy to the World • O Holy Night • Silver and Gold • Suzy Snowflake • and more. Does not include TAB.
00698978 Easy Guitar $17.99

CHRISTMAS
INCLUDES TAB

Guitar Play-Along Volume 22
Book/Online Audio
8 songs: The Christmas Song (Chestnuts Roasting on an Open Fire) • Frosty the Snow Man • Happy Xmas (War Is Over) • Here Comes Santa Claus (Right Down Santa Claus Lane) • Jingle-Bell Rock • Merry Christmas, Darling • Rudolph the Red-Nosed Reindeer • Silver Bells.
00699600 Guitar Tab $15.99

CHRISTMAS CAROLS

Guitar Chord Songbook
80 favorite carols for guitarists who just need the lyrics and chords: Angels We Have Heard on High • Away in a Manger • Deck the Hall • Good King Wenceslas • The Holly and the Ivy • Irish Carol • Jingle Bells • Joy to the World • O Holy Night • Rocking • Silent Night • Up on the Housetop • Welsh Carol • What Child Is This? • and more.
00699536 Lyrics/Chord Symbols/
         Guitar Chord Diagrams $12.99

CHRISTMAS CAROLS
INCLUDES TAB

Guitar Play-Along Volume 62
Book/CD Pack
8 songs: God Rest Ye Merry, Gentlemen • Hark! The Herald Angels Sing • It Came upon the Midnight Clear • O Come, All Ye Faithful (Adeste Fideles) • O Holy Night • Silent Night • We Three Kings of Orient Are • What Child Is This?
00699798 Guitar Tab $12.95

CHRISTMAS CAROLS
INCLUDES TAB

Jazz Guitar Chord Melody Solos
Chord melody arrangements in notes & tab of 26 songs of the season. Includes: Auld Lang Syne • Deck the Hall • Good King Wenceslas • Here We Come A-Wassailing • Joy to the World • O Little Town of Bethlehem • Toyland • We Three Kings of Orient Are • and more.
00701697 Solo Guitar $12.99

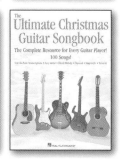

THE CHRISTMAS GUITAR COLLECTION
INCLUDES TAB

Book/CD Pack
20 beautiful fingerstyle arrangements of contemporary Christmas favorites, including: Blue Christmas • Feliz Navidad • Happy Xmas (War Is Over) • I Saw Mommy Kissing Santa Claus • I'll Be Home for Christmas • A Marshmallow World • The Most Wonderful Time of the Year • What Are You Doing New Year's Eve? • and more. CD includes full demos of each piece.
00700181 Fingerstyle Guitar $17.95

CLASSICAL GUITAR CHRISTMAS COLLECTION
INCLUDES TAB

Includes classical guitar arrangements in standard notation and tablature for more than two dozen beloved carols: Angels We Have Heard on High • Auld Lang Syne • Ave Maria • Away in a Manger • Canon in D • The First Noel • I Saw Three Ships • Joy to the World • O Christmas Tree • O Holy Night • Silent Night • What Child Is This? • and more.
00699493 Guitar Solo $10.99

FINGERPICKING CHRISTMAS
INCLUDES TAB

Features 20 classic carols for the intermediate-level guitarist. Includes: Away in a Manger • Deck the Hall • The First Noel • It Came upon the Midnight Clear • Jingle Bells • O Come, All Ye Faithful • Silent Night • We Wish You a Merry Christmas • What Child Is This? • and more.
00699599 Solo Guitar $9.99

FINGERPICKING YULETIDE
INCLUDES TAB

Carefully written for intermediate-level guitarists, this collection includes an introduction to fingerstyle guitar and 16 holiday favorites: Do You Hear What I Hear • Happy Xmas (War Is Over) • A Holly Jolly Christmas • Jingle-Bell Rock • Rudolph the Red-Nosed Reindeer • and more.
00699654 Fingerstyle Guitar $9.99

FIRST 50 CHRISTMAS CAROLS YOU SHOULD PLAY ON GUITAR
INCLUDES TAB

Accessible, must-know Christmas songs are included in this collection arranged for guitar solo with a combo of tab, chords and lyrics. Includes: Angels We Have Heard on High • The First Noel • God Rest Ye Merry, Gentlemen • The Holly and the Ivy • O Christmas Tree • Silent Night • Up on the Housetop • What Child Is This? • and more.
00236224 Guitar Solo $12.99

THE ULTIMATE CHRISTMAS GUITAR SONGBOOK

100 songs in a variety of notation styles, from easy guitar and classical guitar arrangements to note-for-note guitar tab transcriptions. Includes: All Through the Night • Auld Lang Syne • Away in a Manger • Blue Christmas • The Chipmunk Song • The Gift • I've Got My Love to Keep Me Warm • Jingle Bells • One Bright Star • Santa Baby • Silver Bells • Wonderful Christmastime • and more.
00700185 Multi-Arrangements $19.95

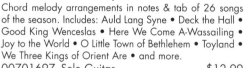

0518

EASY GUITAR WITH NOTES & TAB

This series features simplified arrangements with notes, tab, chord charts, and strum and pick patterns.

MIXED FOLIOS

00702287	Acoustic	$16.99
00702002	Acoustic Rock Hits for Easy Guitar	$15.99
00702166	All-Time Best Guitar Collection	$19.99
00702232	Best Acoustic Songs for Easy Guitar	$14.99
00119835	Best Children's Songs	$16.99
00702233	Best Hard Rock Songs	$15.99
00703055	The Big Book of Nursery Rhymes & Children's Songs	$16.99
00322179	The Big Easy Book of Classic Rock Guitar	$24.95
00698978	Big Christmas Collection	$17.99
00702394	Bluegrass Songs for Easy Guitar	$12.99
00289632	Bohemian Rhapsody	$17.99
00703387	Celtic Classics	$14.99
00224808	Chart Hits of 2016-2017	$14.99
00267383	Chart Hits of 2017-2018	$14.99
00702149	Children's Christian Songbook	$9.99
00702028	Christmas Classics	$8.99
00101779	Christmas Guitar	$14.99
00702185	Christmas Hits	$10.99
00702141	Classic Rock	$8.95
00159642	Classical Melodies	$12.99
00253933	Disney/Pixar's Coco	$16.99
00702203	CMT's 100 Greatest Country Songs	$29.99
00702283	The Contemporary Christian Collection	$16.99
00196954	Contemporary Disney	$16.99
00702239	Country Classics for Easy Guitar	$22.99
00702257	Easy Acoustic Guitar Songs	$14.99
00702280	Easy Guitar Tab White Pages	$29.99
00702041	Favorite Hymns for Easy Guitar	$10.99
00222701	Folk Pop Songs	$14.99
00140841	4-Chord Hymns for Guitar	$9.99
00702281	4 Chord Rock	$10.99
00126894	Frozen	$14.99
00702286	Glee	$16.99
00699374	Gospel Favorites	$16.99
00702160	The Great American Country Songbook	$16.99
00702050	Great Classical Themes for Easy Guitar	$8.99
00702116	Greatest Hymns for Guitar	$10.99
00275088	The Greatest Showman	$17.99
00148030	Halloween Guitar Songs	$14.99
00702273	Irish Songs	$12.99
00192503	Jazz Classics for Easy Guitar	$14.99
00702275	Jazz Favorites for Easy Guitar	$15.99
00702274	Jazz Standards for Easy Guitar	$16.99
00702162	Jumbo Easy Guitar Songbook	$19.99
00232285	La La Land	$16.99
00702258	Legends of Rock	$14.99
00702189	MTV's 100 Greatest Pop Songs	$24.95
00702272	1950s Rock	$15.99
00702271	1960s Rock	$15.99
00702270	1970s Rock	$16.99
00702269	1980s Rock	$15.99
00702268	1990s Rock	$19.99
00109725	Once	$14.99
00702187	Selections from O Brother Where Art Thou?	$17.99
00702178	100 Songs for Kids	$14.99
00702515	Pirates of the Caribbean	$14.99
00702125	Praise and Worship for Guitar	$10.99
00287930	Songs from *A Star Is Born, The Greatest Showman, La La Land*, and More Movie Musicals	$16.99
00702285	Southern Rock Hits	$12.99
00156420	Star Wars Music	$14.99
00121535	30 Easy Celtic Guitar Solos	$15.99
00702220	Today's Country Hits	$12.99
00121900	Today's Women of Pop & Rock	$14.99
00244654	Top Hits of 2017	$14.99
00283786	Top Hits of 2018	$14.99
00702294	Top Worship Hits	$15.99
00702255	VH1's 100 Greatest Hard Rock Songs	$27.99
00702175	VH1's 100 Greatest Songs of Rock and Roll	$24.99
00702253	Wicked	$12.99

ARTIST COLLECTIONS

00702267	AC/DC for Easy Guitar	$15.99
00702598	Adele for Easy Guitar	$15.99
00156221	Adele – 25	$16.99
00702040	Best of the Allman Brothers	$16.99
00702865	J.S. Bach for Easy Guitar	$14.99
00702169	Best of The Beach Boys	$12.99
00702292	The Beatles — 1	$19.99
00125796	Best of Chuck Berry	$15.99
00702201	The Essential Black Sabbath	$12.95
02501615	Zac Brown Band — The Foundation	$16.99
02501621	Zac Brown Band — You Get What You Give	$16.99
00702043	Best of Johnny Cash	$16.99
00702090	Eric Clapton's Best	$12.99
00702086	Eric Clapton — from the Album Unplugged	$15.99
00702202	The Essential Eric Clapton	$14.99
00702250	blink-182 — Greatest Hits	$15.99
00702053	Best of Patsy Cline	$15.99
00222697	Very Best of Coldplay – 2nd Edition	$14.99
00702229	The Very Best of Creedence Clearwater Revival	$15.99
00702145	Best of Jim Croce	$15.99
00702278	Crosby, Stills & Nash	$12.99
14042809	Bob Dylan	$14.99
00702276	Fleetwood Mac — Easy Guitar Collection	$14.99
00139462	The Very Best of Grateful Dead	$15.99
00702136	Best of Merle Haggard	$14.99
00702227	Jimi Hendrix — Smash Hits	$16.99
00702288	Best of Hillsong United	$12.99
00702236	Best of Antonio Carlos Jobim	$14.99
00702245	Elton John — Greatest Hits 1970–2002	$17.99
00129855	Jack Johnson	$16.99
00702204	Robert Johnson	$10.99
00702234	Selections from Toby Keith — 35 Biggest Hits	$12.95
00702003	Kiss	$12.99
00702216	Lynyrd Skynyrd	$15.99
00702182	The Essential Bob Marley	$14.99
00146081	Maroon 5	$14.99
00121925	Bruno Mars – Unorthodox Jukebox	$12.99
00702248	Paul McCartney — All the Best	$14.99
00702129	Songs of Sarah McLachlan	$12.95
00125484	The Best of MercyMe	$12.99
02501316	Metallica — Death Magnetic	$19.99
00702209	Steve Miller Band — Young Hearts (Greatest Hits)	$12.95
00124167	Jason Mraz	$15.99
00702096	Best of Nirvana	$15.99
00702211	The Offspring — Greatest Hits	$12.95
00138026	One Direction	$14.99
00702030	Best of Roy Orbison	$15.99
00702144	Best of Ozzy Osbourne	$14.99
00702279	Tom Petty	$12.99
00102911	Pink Floyd	$16.99
00702139	Elvis Country Favorites	$16.99
00702293	The Very Best of Prince	$15.99
00699415	Best of Queen for Guitar	$15.99
00109279	Best of R.E.M.	$14.99
00702208	Red Hot Chili Peppers — Greatest Hits	$15.99
00198960	The Rolling Stones	$16.99
00174793	The Very Best of Santana	$14.99
00702196	Best of Bob Seger	$12.95
00146046	Ed Sheeran	$14.99
00702252	Frank Sinatra — Nothing But the Best	$12.99
00702010	Best of Rod Stewart	$16.99
00702049	Best of George Strait	$14.99
00702259	Taylor Swift for Easy Guitar	$15.99
00254499	Taylor Swift – Easy Guitar Anthology	$19.99
00702260	Taylor Swift — Fearless	$14.99
00139727	Taylor Swift — 1989	$17.99
00115960	Taylor Swift — Red	$16.99
00253667	Taylor Swift — Reputation	$17.99
00702290	Taylor Swift — Speak Now	$16.99
00232849	Chris Tomlin Collection – 2nd Edition	$14.99
00702226	Chris Tomlin — See the Morning	$12.95
00148643	Train	$14.99
00702427	U2 — 18 Singles	$16.99
00702108	Best of Stevie Ray Vaughan	$16.99
00279005	The Who	$14.99
00702123	Best of Hank Williams	$14.99
00194548	Best of John Williams	$14.99
00702111	Stevie Wonder — Guitar Collection	$9.95
00702228	Neil Young — Greatest Hits	$15.99
00119133	Neil Young — Harvest	$14.99

Prices, contents and availability subject to change without notice.

HAL•LEONARD®

Visit Hal Leonard online at **halleonard.com**

0819
306